Reviews of Selected Published Tests in English

# Reviews of Selected Published Tests in English

National Council of Teachers of English
1111 Kenyon Road, Urbana, Illinois 61801

Prepared by the NCTE Committee to Review Standardized Tests,
Alfred H. Grommon, Chairman.

NCTE EDITORIAL BOARD   Charles E. Cooper, Evelyn Copeland,
Bernice E. Cullinan, Richard Lloyd-Jones, Frank Zidonis,
Robert F. Hogan, *ex officio*, Paul O'Dea, *ex officio*.

BOOK DESIGN   Bob Bingenheimer

ISBN 0-8141-4121-8
NCTE Stock Number 41218

Library of Congress Cataloging in Publication Data

NCTE Committee to Review Standardized Tests.
   Reviews of selected published tests in English.

   Includes bibliographical references and index.
   1.   English philology--Study and teaching--United
States.   2.   Educational tests and measurements.
I.   Grommon, Alfred H.   II.   Braddock, Richard Reed.
III.   Title.                                              15Feb'78
PE68.U5N2   1976      420'.7'6            75-26123
ISDN 0-8141-4121-8

# Contents

# Introduction

*Alfred H. Grommon*

As a consequence of their involvement in systems of educational accountability throughout the nation, English teachers are perforce encountering uses of standardized tests of some kind. Considerable evidence indicates widespread interest, but mostly genuine concern, among teachers of English about uses of standardized tests related to aspects of English programs in schools. According to Leon Lessinger, over 4,000 books and articles on accountability were published between 1970 and 1974 ("Holding the Accountability Movement Accountable," *Phi Delta Kappan* 55 [June 1974], p. 657). Most plans of statewide testing and assessment now functioning include some form of standardized testing of aspects of English grammar, sentence structure, usage, vocabulary, effectiveness of written expression, punctuation, capitalization, spelling, and literature. The majority also include tests of reading skills.

Questions about the purposes of testing programs and the selection of tests continue to arise among teachers using standardized tests presumably designed to yield meaningful information about pupils' knowledge of and skills in using the English language and in reading literature. Just what are the purposes of these extensive testing programs? Who selects the tests? What criteria are applied in choosing tests? How valid is the content of each of these instruments? How representative of outcomes of the entire program of English are the results of tests focused upon limited segments of such a complex subject? How are results to be used in accounting to the public and to educational agencies and authorities and in making state and local decisions about educational policies? What effects may test results have upon the status of individual teachers and upon states' allocations of funds to public schools in general and to a school district or school in particular?

1

Because of these questions and other related problems, the National Council of Teachers of English has for some time been concerned with the nature, uses, and misuses of standardized tests. The Council has been interested especially in two major questions:

(1) What is the validity of the subject-matter content of standardized English tests; that is, what is the relation between what is known now about the subject of English, and the teaching of it, and the conceptions of it explicitly or implicitly underlying the format of, and subject-matter items in, such tests?

(2) How representative of the larger outcomes of the purposes and breadth of a school's total program of English are results of a standardized test designed to produce information about pupils' knowledge and skills related to only a small segment of the subject?

To inform the profession and the public about the nature and scope of English as a school subject and about the teaching of it, the Council—almost from its inception in 1911—has been publishing articles, monographs, books, reports presenting results of inquiries into many aspects of the subject.

Legislators, state and local school administrators, parents, and teachers committed to using standardized tests as a means of appraising pupils' English skills should be informed also on such NCTE publications. Any decisions about the purposes of testing in English and about the selection of a particular standardized test should be based upon some familiarity with these and other contributions by leaders in the field. The Council's publications are evidence of a long and continuing mission of bringing to the profession the best scholarly research available, representative points of view, and stimulating accounts of experiences in the teaching of English. All constitute an overview of the scope of English in the schools and create a much larger construct of English than can be reflected in any standardized tests of small parts of pupils' experiences with this subject. The Council's publications, cited in a chronological list of Selected References at the end of this Introduction, provide a background against which any uses of standardized and other forms of tests, including the interpretation and uses of their results, should be considered carefully.

As the publications indicate, the Council has been giving continued attention to the nationwide insistence upon holding schools accountable to the public for the effectiveness of their educational programs and their teaching and the accompanying uses of standardized tests in English. These publications, including this one, are an outgrowth, in part, of the concerns expressed in the following resolutions on accountability and on the use of standardized English tests passed by the NCTE membership at the Annual Business Meeting in November, 1971.

## On Accountability

*Background:* English teachers recognize their accountability to various groups—to students, to colleagues both within and without the discipline of English, to parents, to the local community which supports the schools, and to the wider communities beyond it. However, they reject the view that their goals and objectives can be stated only in quantifiably measurable terms, describing the behavior their students will display at the completion of instruction.

Moreover, just as important as the English teacher's accountability to his students, to his colleagues, and to the communities which have a responsible interest in his activities, is the accountability of each of these groups to him. Students are responsible for being active participants in the learning process. Parents are responsible for supplying a nurturing environment and for being valued colleagues in developing appropriate learning programs. Administrators and others who provide the school climate are responsible for fostering the teaching process. The wider communities are responsible for providing financial, cultural, and social support. It is now part of the English teacher's obligation to clarify for himself, his students, his colleagues, and his several communities how he can be accountable. Be it therefore

**Resolved**, That the National Council of Teachers of English (1) describe the diverse and appropriate ways it is possible to know that students are learning, and (2) recommend the most effective means of communicating this information as well as teachers' expectations about the responsibilities that students, parents, administrators, and the general public have to the educational program of the community.

## On the Use of Standardized Tests

*Background:* Standardized tests of achievement in English and reading have been subjects of growing controversy. Some test norms were established long ago or were based on populations that do not resemble the population being tested. The contents of many tests, moreover, are widely regarded as culturally biased or pertinent to outdated curricula. Moreover, many students who fail to demonstrate reading competency on standardized tests can and do read materials of interest to them.

Clearly other measures than standardized tests are needed to evaluate achievement in language arts skills. These include locally prepared tests of language arts skills, surveys of students' reading habits, and evaluations by teachers who work daily with students. Be it therefore

**Resolved,** That the National Council of Teachers of English urge local school districts, colleges, and state agencies

(1) to re-examine standardized tests of English and reading in order to determine the appropriateness of their content to actual instructional goals and the appropriateness of the test norms to students;

(2) to study problems in the use and interpretation of these tests; and

(3) to consider carefully means other than standardized tests, including student self-evaluation, of assessing the language arts skills of students.

## NCTE Committee to Review Standardized Tests

The Committee on Research of the National Council of Teachers of English appointed an ad hoc committee to examine a wide sampling of English tests commercially prepared and published and readily available to teachers of English, and to prepare a report of reviews written by members of this NCTE Committee to Review Standardized Tests. The reviewers were asked to evaluate only the validity of the content of selected tests. In focusing attention upon the subject matter of each test, the reviewers were concerned with such questions as the following:

(1) What do the format and items of a test reveal about the test-makers' underlying assumptions about and concepts of the English language, of readers' responses to literature, and of the learning and teaching of English?

(2) How valid are these assumptions, concepts, and items in the light of what is known now about the nature of the English language, about current acceptability of a variety of dialects and usages in speaking and writing, about readers' responses to literature, and about teaching English in a pluralistic society?

The reviewers were not concerned with other features such as the national sampling of test-takers, the establishing and revising of norms, reliability, and means of interpreting results.

Part One of this report offers a context for current testing somewhat larger than that represented by an individual teacher's experiences with standardized tests or by a review of a particular test. I have endeavored to clarify what seems to be meant by the term "educational accountability" that occurs in almost every statewide testing program; to identify what appear to be encouraging developments in statewide programs of testing and assessment; and to point out some major problems in English tests, and tests in general, that English teachers should consider. The evaluation of a particular test should be considered also in the larger context presented in Part One.

Part Two offers 58 reviews, the major purpose of this report. These represent evaluations of the content of 51 different tests. Tests of reading skills are not included, however. The introductions to the reviews discuss the kinds of tests examined and the relation of the segment of English tested to an entire program of English; identify some criteria applied to each test; or point out the purposes of the tests, their strengths and weaknesses, and kinds of tests needed. As is immediately apparent, each reviewer was free to make his own judgments and to write his reviews in whatever style he preferred.

Part Three summarizes some of the problems in educational accountability and suggests specific things that teachers can do.

Professor Walter Loban, School of Education, University of California, Berkeley, generally discusses tests intended to produce information about a child's developing competence in using the English language, from preschool through the elementary grades. Professor William A. Jenkins, Academic Vice-President, Florida International University and former editor of *Elementary English*, reviews tests of grammar, usage, diction, punctuation, and spelling prepared principally for grades 4-9. Professor J. N. Hook, Professor of English and Counselor, Council on Teacher Education, Emeritus, University of Illinois, and the first Executive Secretary of the NCTE, reviews tests of grammar, diction, usage, punctuation, and spelling intended primarily for grades 9-12; some forms are also used in the junior high school. In addition, he reviews several tests containing sections on effectiveness of written expression; these reviews are included in the section on writing tests, introduced by the late Professor Richard Braddock, Department of English, University of Iowa. Professor Alan C. Purves, College of Education, University of Illinois, reviews tests of knowledge about, interpretation of, and responses to litera-ture. Professor Dan Donlan, University of California, Riverside, re-views one sequence of tests on literature.

Although the NCTE Committee to Review Standardized Tests tried to make a rather thorough search of tests available to teachers of English, it makes no claim to having reviewed every English test described in publishers' catalogs. Instead, it selected a broad range of instruments that seemed to be in wide use in schools.

The work of the NCTE Committee to Review Standardized Tests, now completed, will be extended through the charges given to the NCTE Task Force on Measurement and Evaluation in the Study of English and the NCTE Committee to Study the National Assessment of Educational Progress. These appointments further manifest the Council's involvement with implications of the expanding uses of assessment in English.

I wish to thank Professors Hook, Jenkins, Loban, Purves, and Donlan for their many valuable contributions to this report. I wish to thank also Dr. James R. Squire, former chairman of the Commit-tee on Research, and Professor Purves, also a former member of the Committee, who originally suggested that reviews of English tests be published by the Council and who initiated, planned, and nourished the project culminating in this report.

## Selected References

1932    Leonard, Sterling A. *Current English Usage*. English Mono-graph No. 1 of the National Council of Teachers of English. Chicago: The Inland Press.

1938    Marckwardt, Albert H., and Walcott, Fred G. *Facts about Current English Usage*. English Monograph No. 7 of the Na-tional Council of Teachers of English. New York: D. Ap-pleton-Century Company.

1940    Fries, Charles C. *American English Grammar*. English Monograph No. 10 of the National Council of Teachers of English. New York: D. Appleton-Century Company.

1946    Pooley, Robert C. *Teaching English Usage*. English Mono-graph No. 16 of the National Council of Teachers of English. New York: Appleton-Century-Crofts, Inc.

1952    NCTE Commission on the English Curriculum. *The English Language Arts*. Curriculum Series Vol. I. New York: Apple-ton-Century-Crofts, Inc.

1954   NCTE Commission on the English Curriculum. *Language Arts for Today's Children.* Curriculum Series Vol. II. New York: Appleton-Century-Crofts, Inc.

1956   NCTE Commission on the English Curriculum. *The English Language Arts in the Secondary School.* Curriculum Series Vol. III. New York: Appleton-Century-Crofts, Inc.

1963   Braddock, Richard, Lloyd-Jones, Richard, and Schoer, Lowell. *Research in Written Composition.* Urbana, Ill.: National Council of Teachers of English.

1963   Loban, Walter D. *The Language of Elementary School Children.* Research Report No. 1. Urbana, Ill.: National Council of Teachers of English.

1965   NCTE Task Force on Teaching English to the Disadvantaged. *Language Programs for the Disadvantaged.* Edited by Richard Corbin and Muriel Crosby. Urbana, Ill.: National Council of Teachers of English.

1965   Hunt, Kellogg W. *Grammatical Structures Written at Three Grade Levels.* Research Report No. 3. Urbana, Ill.: National Council of Teachers of English.

1965   Judine, Sister M., I.H.M. *A Guide for Evaluating Student Composition.* Urbana, Ill.: National Council of Teachers of English.

1966   Bateman, Donald R., and Zidonis, Frank J. *The Effect of a Study of Transformational Grammar on the Writing of Ninth and Tenth Graders.* Research Report No. 6. Urbana, Ill.: National Council of Teachers of English.

1966   Committee on the National Conference on Research in English. *Research on Handwriting and Spelling.* Edited by Thomas D. Horn. Urbana, Ill.: National Council of Teachers of English.

1966   Loban, Walter. *Problems in Oral English.* Research Report No. 5. Urbana, Ill.: National Council of Teachers of English.

1967   Board of Education of the City of New York. *Nonstandard Dialect.* Urbana, Ill.: National Council of Teachers of English.

1967   O'Donnell, Roy C., Griffin, William J., and Norris, Raymond C. *Syntax of Kindergarten and Elementary School*

*Children: A Transformational Analysis.* Research Report No. 8. Urbana, Ill.: National Council of Teachers of English.

1968   Petty, Walter T., Herold, Curtis P., and Stoll, Earline. *The State of Knowledge about the Teaching of Vocabulary.* Urbana, Ill.: National Council of Teachers of English.

1969   Mellon, John C. *Transformational Sentence-Combining: A Method for Enhancing the Development of Syntactic Fluency in English Composition.* Research Report No. 10. Urbana, Ill.: National Council of Teachers of English.

1969   Sherwin, J. Stephen. *Four Problems in Teaching English: A Critique of Research.* Scranton, Pa.: International Textbook Company for the National Council of Teachers of English.

1970   Labov, William. *The Study of Nonstandard English.* Urbana, Ill.: National Council of Teachers of English for the Center for Applied Linguistics.

1970   NCTE Commission on the English Curriculum. *On Writing Behavioral Objectives for English.* Edited by John Maxwell and Anthony Tovatt. Urbana, Ill.: National Council of Teachers of English.

1971   NCTE Commission on Composition. *The Student's Right to Write.* Urbana, Ill.: National Council of Teachers of English.

1971   O'Hare, Frank. *Sentence Combining: Improving Student Writing without Formal Grammar Instruction.* Research Report No. 15. Urbana, Ill.: National Council of Teachers of English.

1972   NCTE Commission on the English Curriculum. *Accountability and the Teaching of English.* Edited by Henry B. Maloney. Urbana, Ill.: National Council of Teachers of English.

1972   Purves, Alan C., and Beach, Richard. *Literature and the Reader: Research in Response to Literature, Reading Interests, and the Teaching of Literature.* Urbana, Ill.: National Council of Teachers of English.

1973   NCTE Commission on Reading. *Accountability and Reading Instruction: Critical Issues.* Edited by Robert B. Ruddell. Urbana, Ill.: National Council of Teachers of English.

1974    Cullinan, Bernice E. *Black Dialects and Reading.* Urbana, Ill.: ERIC Clearinghouse on Reading and Communication Skills and National Council of Teachers of English.

1974    Diederich, Paul B. *Measuring Growth in English.* Urbana, Ill.: National Council of Teachers of English.

1974    Pooley, Robert C. *The Teaching of English Usage.* Urbana, Ill.: National Council of Teachers of English.

1974    *Uses, Abuses, Misuses of Standardized Tests in English: A First-Aid Kit for the Test-Wounded.* Urbana, Ill.: National Council of Teachers of English.

1975    Fagan, William T., Cooper, Charles R., and Jensen, Julie M. *Measures for Research and Evaluation in the English Language Arts.* Urbana, Ill.: ERIC Clearinghouse on Reading and Communication Skills and National Council of Teachers of English.

1975    NCTE Task Force on Measurement and Evaluation in the Study of English. *Common Sense in Testing.* Urbana, Ill.: National Council of Teachers of English.

1975    Mellon, John C. *National Assessment and the Teaching of English.* Urbana, Ill.: National Council of Teachers of English.

1

# Statewide Accountability Programs of Testing and Assessment

*Alfred H. Grommon*

*"Accountability! Accountability!"* "When I use a word," says Humpty Dumpty, "it means just what I choose it to mean—neither more nor less." And apparently so say or imply some persons in state legislatures, state departments of education, and local communities concerned with finding out for some purposes, somehow, something about the effectiveness of programs and teaching in schools for which they feel responsible or in which they have involvement as parents and taxpayers. However educational accountability may be defined or implied, efforts to hold schools accountable to the public and to outside agencies are now nationwide.

The Educational Testing Services (ETS) study, *State Educational Assessment Programs, 1973 Revision,* reports that each of the fifty states, the District of Columbia, Puerto Rico, and the Virgin Islands either had a statewide educational assessment program already in force or had one in the planning stage.[1] ETS also made a follow-up study, *State Testing Programs, 1973 Revision,* of its 1968 survey and found that in 1972-73, thirty-three states had forty-two statewide testing programs functioning, and additional programs were being planned.[2] Unquestionably, mandated programs of educational accountability, in some form, are important components of inquiries into what states are getting for their educational investment.

These programs are not trouble-free. To an increasing number of teachers, "accountability" is a threatening concept and term. Teachers' protests against the accountability movement in education seem to be multiplying. The ETS surveys disclose that a rather common problem experienced by administrators of several programs is the need to reckon with teachers' negative attitudes toward mandatory uses of standardized tests, especially where the results may prove disadvantageous for teachers, their students, and their schools. According to *The New York Times* (July 6, 1974), many of

13

the 10,000 members of the National Education Association (NEA) attending a convention in Chicago expressed their determination "to fight accountability unless the teachers themselves have a key role in the establishment of plans." Terry E. Herndon, executive secretary of the NEA, then having a membership of 1,400,000, was quoted as saying, "Teachers do not—and will not—accept this simplistic, bureaucratic approach to teacher accountability that is prevalent in America today." He suggested that "teachers ought to refuse to give tests that are not found acceptable." The *Times* further reports, "Teacher antagonism toward tests has risen to such heights that the National Education Association has called for a moratorium on all group standardized intelligence, aptitude and achievement tests."

The question of acceptability of standardized tests now being used in English classes has long been a concern of members of the National Council of Teachers of English. This report is one outgrowth of the Council's commitment to bring to the profession information pertinent to urgent educational problems encountered by teachers of English. Many are deeply concerned about statewide and local programs that require the use of standardized English tests as a means of presumably identifying achievement levels in limited aspects of a complex subject. The major purpose of this report is to offer teachers and administrators evaluations of many published English tests and to offer an extended context, about tests and programs of testing and assessment, in which the nature and uses of objective measures may be considered.

Teachers' participation in planning and administering any system of educational accountability is indeed important—and will be commented upon later in this report—but questions arise about what kind of system they might be participating in. For what purposes are programs of accountability designed? In communities consisting of diverse socioeconomic and cultural constituencies, for whose benefit are the programs planned and the results to be used? What effect, if any, will test results have upon state and local decisions on educational policy and upon the status of teachers?

According to Henry M. Levin, the extensive literature of educational accountability indicates "four relatively distinct concepts of accountability: (a) as performance reporting; (b) as a technical process; (c) as a political process; (d) as an institutional process."[3] The kind of accountability considered here is mainly performance reporting.

Results of standardized English tests, along with those of other kinds being used statewide and in local school districts, are reported to such constituencies as governors, state legislatures, state departments of education, local school districts and communities, teachers, and students. Inquiries into the purposes of performance reporting, the relation of accountability to educational goals, the processes by which statewide goals were established—by whom and for whom, the uses of test results, and the kinds of involvement of and consideration given to diverse groups in the community, all such inquiries would seem to lead inevitably into aspects of technical, political, and institutional processes. Inquirers should not overlook positive aspects of plans. According to Frederick McDonald, director of Educational Studies at ETS, "Accountability is too frequently defined in negative terms, with too much emphasis on its punitive interpretations." As reported in *ETS Developments*, McDonald sees "accountability as the acceptance of *responsibility for consequences* by those to whom citizens entrust the performance of certain public services. Thus, in its educational context, an accountability system's primary purpose is to promote student development."[4] Consequently, teachers' participation in any program of educational accountability surely should not be limited to ensuring the selection of acceptable tests. Rather, they should contribute to the entire scope of the program.

Educational accountability involves "testing" and "assessment." Although these terms are used interchangeably in this discussion, the distinctions made in the ETS surveys should be clarified, especially for teachers concerned about their roles in accountability systems. Standardized tests are basic to all statewide testing programs and usually constitute the only kind of measurement provided by the state. While the use of standardized tests may be part of some assessment programs, this use does not circumscribe the scope of an assessment program, since assessments are designed to explore a wide range of educational needs and services throughout a state's public schools.

Henry S. Dyer, while vice president of ETS, stated, "You can have assessment of educational programs and services without any testing at all. You can also have testing without any assessment of educational programs and services."[5] An Oklahoma report, included in the previously cited ETS 1973 assessment survey, also identifies some confusion about these concepts and further clarifies the distinctions made in that state:

One major problem developed and continues: the difficulty encountered in convincing the uninformed (including test makers and the testing company personnel) that needs assessment is not

merely getting results on standardized tests or criterion-referenced test items in the academic or nonacademic areas, but includes the whole range of human needs which may or may not relate to the way our schools are currently operating.[6]

Because the ETS 1973 assessment survey and the Oklahoma report
are referred to frequently in the following discussion, it seems essential to clarify here the distinctions ETS and many states make between the limited nature and purposes of instruments used in statewide programs of testing and the more extensive characteristics of
assessment.

The majority of statewide programs of testing and assessment include efforts to measure the results of the teaching of English, and to
some extent the effectiveness of the teachers and of their English
programs. Thirty-three states, now conducting statewide assessments of educational needs or planning to do so, are or will be
assessing the results of their school programs in what are identified
as language arts, English, grammar, spelling, punctuation, composition or effectiveness of written expression, literature, and speaking.
In addition, forty-seven states are assessing children's needs in reading. Moreover, the ETS 1973 testing survey shows that thirty-two
programs in twenty-seven states also include tests of English and
writing, and thirty-two programs in thirty states test reading skills.
Consequently, there seems to be no way in which English teachers
can avoid being involved with some form of testing, either as a part
of statewide programs or of those in local districts or individual
schools.

## Accountability and Statewide Programs

Uses of any kind of standardized or locally prepared tests should be
considered within the larger context of what is generally called "accountability." As indicated earlier, all the states, the District of
Columbia, Puerto Rico, and the Virgin Islands are now either administering programs of testing and assessment or planning to insti-
tute them. All systems are intended to produce information about
aspects of education in public schools for which the local community, state department of education, or the state legislature is
holding the schools accountable, in one form or another.

In his article, *Evaluation, Decision-Making, and Accountability*,
Garlie A. Forehand differentiates between evaluation and accountability and their relation to the making of educational decisions. In

his view, evaluation "consists of gathering, processing, and using information about each element [in the process of curriculum development: goals, procedures, implementation, feedback]. It takes place throughout the cycle. Evaluation is an ongoing activity, rather than a single one-shot study, an aid to decision-making rather than a summary judgment, a rational procedure rather than a routinized program." Comparing and contrasting evaluation and accountability, Forehand states:

> Now, in the early 1970's, evaluation has acquired a still different and still new guise, which goes by the name of accountability. Many of the characteristics and techniques of the other concepts of evaluation are retained in this newer version. The value of a program is to be measured by its effects on the performance of students. The technique of defining behavioral objectives—educational goals translated into objectively observable behaviors—is used to assess goals and their attainment. Results are to be assessed in comparison to predefined standards. *The main difference between accountability and other concepts of evaluation lies in the relationship posited between the public (usually as represented by political bodies) and the educator.* Accountability assumes the relationship to be a contractual one. . . . In general, at least in the discussions of accountability most commonly encountered thus far, the methods for achieving the objectives are not part of the contract, save, by assumption, in unstated ethical strictures. As compared to other concepts of evaluation discussed here, accountability is relatively far removed from considerations of method, theory, hypothesis, and concept. . . .
>
> Traditional evaluation for course improvement is carried out by the development team, emphasizing formative questions for the purpose of revising procedures. Evaluation of new curricula may be carried out from any perspective; it generally emphasizes summative evaluation for the purpose of making decisions about adoption or support. *Accountability generally takes the perspective of the public—concentrates on the evaluation of end products, and is conducted for the purpose of learning the extent to which the teacher or school has met obligations.*[7]

The central importance of the public's involvement in programs of testing and assessment is plainly stated also in the ETS 1973 assessment survey: "Accountability is the heart and soul of most assessment programs. More importantly, state education agencies in every state in the union are taking the leadership in helping or coercing school administrators to answer to the public's cries for better information about what children know and how well schools are doing their job." This analysis of the state's role in programs of accountability continues:

The issue should not be one of state-imposed accountability versus locally initiated accountability. State education agencies and state legislatures have their own reasons and suffer their own pressures for collecting information about students' educational achievements. School districts' accountability to the state should not be confused with school districts' accountability to their own communities or with teachers' accountability to their own school systems.

The issue should be whether state-imposed accountability systems encourage or discourage school administrators and teachers from developing their own accountability plans.

It can be said that accountability laws are the signs of the public's lack of faith in the effectiveness of schooling. It can be said, also, that accountability laws are the signs that school officials did not, or could not, respond on their own to accountability demands.[8]

Because accountability to the public about schools' effectiveness is altogether too general a statement of purpose for statewide testing, ETS questionnaires included items directed at statements of more specific purposes and uses of results of tests. The following summaries of responses to questions are taken from the ETS *State Testing Programs, 1973 Revision* (pp. 2-3,7):

Question 2.  What is the major purpose of the program?
(42 programs in 33 states responding)

| | Program | States |
|---|---|---|
| 1.  Instructional evaluation | 27 | 23 |
| 2.  Identification of individual problems and talents | 23 | 19 |
| 3.  Guidance | 22 | 20 |
| 4.  Provide data for a management information system | 14 | 14 |
| 5.  Placement and grouping | 14 | 13 |

Question 19. · How·are the results of the program used?
(42 programs in 33 states responding)

|    | Program | States |
| --- | --- | --- |
| 1. Instruction | 28 | 24 |
| 2. Program evaluation | 26 | 22 |
| 3. Program planning | 26 | 23 |
| 4. Guidance | 23 | 22 |
| 5. Comparative analysis across schools | 14 | 13 |

The most common goal is to evaluate instruction. When asked about uses of data resulting from tests, the states indicate, again, that the most common use is to evaluate the quality of instruction and of educational programs in public schools. And yet, ETS found in its survey of *State Educational Assessment Programs, 1973 Revision* (p. 7), that only Pennsylvania reported collecting information about teachers' methods of instruction. Moreover, Forehand's statement quoted earlier indicates that, based upon current discussions of accountability, "accountability is relatively far removed from considerations of method, theory, hypothesis, and concept."

ETS also included in its state testing survey (pp. 2-3) an inquiry about methods the states use to inform local schools about test results and the interpretation of them:

Question 20.  What efforts are undertaken to assist local interpretation and use of program results?
(42 programs in 33 states responding)

|    | Programs | States |
| --- | --- | --- |
| 1. Workshops | 31 | 30 |
| 2. Consulting | 26 | 25 |
| 3. Publications | 24 | 21 |
| 4. Audio-visual aids | 11 | 11 |
| 5. Nothing | 5 | 2 |

Question 22.  For whom is this assistance provided?
(37 programs in 33 states responding)

|    | Programs | States |
| --- | --- | --- |
| 1. Administrators | 32 | 29 |
| 2. Classroom teachers | 26 | 25 |
| 3. Guidance counselors | 25 | 25 |
| 4. School boards | 10 | 10 |
| 5. Community groups | 8 | 8 |
| 6. PTA | 6 | 6 |
| 7. Students | 5 | 5 |

Evidently, most states provide local school administrators, teachers, counselors, and board members with information about and implications of the results of statewide tests. Yet little seems to be done to provide the same kinds of information to nonschool members of local communities, even though a major feature of educational accountability programs is the reporting of information about local schools to the local community as well as to the larger community. The following quoted question and comment also are related to the pervasive problem of communication:

Question 24. Who receives a copy of the program reports?
(40 programs in 33 states responding)

|  | Programs | States |
|---|---|---|
| 1.  Schools | 31 | 28 |
| 2.  School districts | 27 | 25 |
| 3.  State Education Agency | 23 | 21 |
| 4.  Students | 20 | 14 |
| 5.  Principals | 17 | 16 |
| 6.  State Board of Education | 16 | 16 |
| 7.  Teachers | 15 | 14 |
| 8.  Colleges or universities | 12 | 11 |
| 9.  Newspapers | 11 | 11 |
| 10.  Governor or Legislature | 8 | 8 |

Only seven programs in seven states report that parents are given reports of results and only six programs in six states distribute reports to the general public . . . most often only upon request. Tying this with the information from question 22, one can conclude that little assistance in the interpretation and use of program results is provided for nonprofessional members of the community *and* the results of programs are not often shared with these individuals.[9]

In addition, about twenty of the states operating statewide assessment programs send reports to the Educational Resources Information Center (ERIC).

Although many states evidently intend to report generally the results of their testing programs, the fact is that those most directly involved in educational programs—students, teachers, and parents—rarely receive test results. Despite the proclaimed top priority given in responses to questions 2 and 19—the evaluation and improvement of instruction and programs—teachers learn of only half of the results reported to schools and school districts. In many states, parents get reports only by requesting them.

The primary emphasis given by many states to tests as a means to evaluate instruction was of some concern to the ETS survey staff because this objective may be based upon questionable assumptions:

> It is probably safe to say that statewide assessment will not produce any startling revelations about what can be done by teachers with pupils to help children learn more effectively. The conclusion is not meant to be as much an indictment of statewide assessment as it is a statement of its limitations. Revelations in teaching practices and methods can come only from intensive analysis within each school building and within each classroom. If statewide assessment data can whet the appetites of teachers and administrators for doing the kinds of evaluation only they can do for themselves, statewide assessment will serve its purposes well.[10]

To draw attention to the importance of helping schools make local decisions, the ETS staff classified state assessment programs into three groups: the seventeen programs designed to collect information to be used in making decisions at the state level; the thirteen programs designed to collect information to be used mainly to help local districts make decisions; and those programs only beginning to emerge in twenty-four other states.

R. E. Stake, a writer on laws of educational accountability, also questions the effectiveness of such laws in improving the quality of education in local schools:

> Most state accountability proposals call for more uniform standards across the state, greater prespecification of objectives, more careful analysis of learning sequences and better testing of student performances. . . . *If state accountability laws are to be in the best interests of the people, they should protect local control of the schools, individuality of teachers, and diversity of learning opportunities.* They should not escalate the bureaucracy at the state or local level. They should not allow school ineffectiveness to be more easily ignored by drawing attention to student performance. They should not permit test scores to be overly influential in schoolwide or personal decisions—the irreducible errors of test scores should be recognized. The laws should make it easier for a school to be accountable to the community in providing a variety of high quality learning opportunities for every learner.[11]

Whatever educational benefits result from statewide testing depend mainly upon the awareness of local school and district administrators, an awareness that they are being held accountable to teachers—as is stated in the NCTE resolution on accountability—and for sharing test results with the teachers and students. If the quality of programs and instruction is to be thereby improved, then administrators must provide teachers and students with some interpretations of results and some local implications. Moreover, they must ensure the involvement, in a major way, of their teachers in any consequent inservice activities intended to improve programs and instruction.

Furthermore, teachers as well as administrators should participate in the preparation of any reports to the local community. English teachers, for example, can make sure that test results are appropriately related to particular parts of their English courses and, even more importantly, that tests are measured against the context of the entire English program in local schools.In so doing, English teachers can awaken the community to another aspect of accountability basic to that NCTE resolution: the relationship of students' performances to the larger educational environment resulting from the degree of awareness that students, parents, local and wider communities seem to have of their being, in turn, accountable to teachers in their schools.

## Trends in Statewide Programs

Lest the preceding discussion seem to emphasize unduly the negative features of educational accountability and of statewide programs of testing and assessment, attention should be given to the positive aspects reported in the ETS surveys. Some merits of statewide programs emerge from a consideration of them in a context larger than an individual teacher's experiences with administering standardized tests in the classroom.

For the sake of assessment, states had to formulate educational goals, applicable statewide. Consideration had to be given to such questions as:

What learning should be achieved by the full range of pupils throughout the public schools in the entire state?

Who should determine what each child's goals should be?

For what purposes and by what means are each child's educational needs and achievements to be assessed?

How are the results of assessment to be used?

According to the ETS 1973 survey of state assessment programs, forty-three states already had established educational goals; the other seven were in the process of doing so. These goals, ranging from one to seventy-eight in the various states, were classified into three groups by ETS: (1) goals identifying desired outcomes for the learner; (2) those related to such processes as having students and other citizens participate in developing curricula; and (3) those involving such institutional matters as standards for personnel, teaching materials, and educational programs. Apparently educational authorities in many states had not engaged previously in an exercise common to teachers: identifying and writing objectives. But the moment a state decided to establish programs of assessment, the first obligatory step was the formulation of educational goals acceptable to a representative segment of concerned people in the state.

Another positive aspect evidenced by the goals of, and tests used in, assessment programs is that most states no longer consider schools and the individual teacher responsible for teaching solely the traditional three "Rs." Instead, many goals represent an explicit concern with the individual pupil's physical, emotional, social, and intellectual development. The ETS survey provides considerable evidence of the extensive efforts to ascertain what is happening in the affective, noncognitive domain of pupils' experiences in school. In some states, in fact, the emphasis upon the affective domain is so pronounced that some people in those states have inferred that perhaps the cognitive, traditional skills are not receiving enough attention. The ETS staff grouped the objectives taken from the states' goals into the following categories, which indicate clearly the emphasis now being given to the affective domain of educational experiences (*Assessment Programs*, p. 6):

1. Basic Skills
2. Cultural Appreciation
3. Self-realization
4. Citizenship and Political Understanding
5. Human Relations
6. Economic Understanding
7. Physical Environment
8. Mental and Physical Health
9. Creative, Constructive and Critical Thinking
10. Career Education and Occupational Competence
11. Lifelong Learning
12. Values and Ethics
13. Home and Family Relations

To these categories, add the following from the ETS testing survey (*Testing Programs*, p. 5):

Question 11.  Which of the following noncognitive areas
are being tested?
(9 programs in 9 states responding)

| | ELEMENTARY | | SECONDARY | |
| | 6 | 6 | 5 | 5 |
| | Programs | States | Programs | States |
| 1. Attitudes toward school | 5 | 5 | 2 | 2 |
| 2. Self-concept | 4 | 4 | 1 | 1 |
| 3. School plans and aspirations | 2 | 2 | 1 | 1 |
| 4. Interests | 1 | 1 | 4 | 4 |
| 5. Biographical data | — | — | 2 | 2 |

For English teachers whose only encounters with standardized tests may be with those aimed at pupils' abilities to punctuate, capitalize, and spell, these examples of widespread attempts to assess noncognitive experiences and attitudes may be encouraging. Evident, too, are the many opportunities English teachers have to contribute significantly to helping pupils attain affective goals. The increasing sophistication in assessing elements of pupils' affective experiences in school may lead to improved instruments—some created by the teachers themselves—for helping teachers and students explore aspects of noncognitive learning. Teachers who have reservations about the relation of statewide programs to pupils' affective experiences in English programs should inquire about the goals of their own state's report.

A third encouraging trend in states' development of educational goals is the use of citizen advisory groups, teachers, and students; the use of statements prepared by citizens in statewide meetings; and the use of research on why and how students learn. Connecticut reports, for example, that "thousands of citizens" contributed to the development of goals for its schools. Kansas reports that in addition to the participation of students, lay citizens, and professional consultants, "approximately 8,000 teachers" contributed to the establishment of goals—one of which stresses the "need to involve lay citizens and students in the planning of the school's curriculum." Approximately 120,000 people in Ohio reviewed and refined the goals for that state. Other states drawing upon citizens, teachers, and students include Florida, Georgia, Nebraska, New Jersey, Rhode Island, Utah, and Wisconsin.

To facilitate the involvement of citizens, California published a three-volume guide, *Education for the People*, to be used in local communities. The guide presents models of how community representatives can participate in creating educational goals appropriate to schools in their community. During 1974, the community goals from throughout the state were to become the basis for establishing an approved set of goals for the entire state.

Thus, the states' decisions to embark upon programs of educational accountability led to their establishment of statewide goals and then of design instruments to identify what the schools were contributing to pupils' progress toward reaching these goals. In the process, state boards of education and other educational authorities drew upon recommendations made by thousands of teachers and students; labor, business, and professional representatives; and specialists from universities, colleges, and community colleges. Whatever effects statewide programs of testing and assessment may have otherwise produced throughout the schools, the states should be credited with accelerating widespread participation of teachers, students, and lay citizens in creating a range of cognitive and affective goals for all pupils in public schools.

A fourth positive development reflected in the ETS surveys is that an increasing number of states are either already using standardized tests "tailor-made" to fit identifiable circumstances or are in the process of creating such tests. This relates directly to the teachers' reservations about, and objections to, the use of commercially prepared standardized tests. Many doubt that any standardized test can fit the circumstances of an individual child, or indeed the characteristics of a particular class or community, and can measure effectively a pupil's English language skills and his or her relationships with literature.

The problem is stated explicitly in the ETS assessment report on the program in Alaska, *Alaska Educational Assessment and Model of Reasonable Expectation*, and reflects an enlightened point of view:

Alaska has elected to design their first statewide assessment of student skills with tests that are culturally free in relation to content and linguistically equivalent in relation to question wording. There are 30 school districts in the state, one of which is under state control. This district consists of 126 rural villages in which seven different Eskimo dialects are spoken in addition to three major Indian dialects and standard American English. The issue is further compounded in that students range from those who are genuinely bilingual to those who are nonlingual (that is, they do not have an adequate command of either the ancestral language or the English language).[12]

Does any standardized test now exist that is appropriate to language abilities and educational needs of these diverse Alaskan pupils, their teachers, their school, and their communities?

The ETS 1973 testing survey shows that of the "41 programs in 32 states, 20 programs in 20 states use only tests purchased 'as is' from test publishers." But of importance here is that "thirteen programs in seven states use only tests which have been tailor-made, and in eight programs in eight states, a combination of purchased tailored, or revised measures is used." In response to the question about who developed these tailor-made tests, the respondents for 21 programs in 13 states reported the following, in descending order of frequency: state education agency, committee of professionals, college or university, test publisher, and outside contractor.[13]

In Part Three of this book, the process used in California to facilitate the development of tailored tests for English will be described as an example of steps other communities may wish to consider in planning procedures for developing or acquiring tests suited to their educational goals and to the learning environment and styles of their pupils.

Present information indicates, then, that either as a result of, or concurrent with, the mandating of statewide programs of testing and assessment, state and local communities are striving to obtain or create tests especially suited to local circumstances. Moreover, further evidence emerging from the ETS surveys indicates that this trend certainly will continue. In responding to the question about which of nine elements in their programs are most likely to change in the near future, representatives of 29 programs in 26 states reported that the tests now being used are the most likely to change.[14]

Standardized or norm-referenced tests certainly have their place in a program in which the student, parent, teacher, school, district, and state want to know how an individual student, class, school, or district compares in certain educational knowledge and skills with other students in the nation. It is useful also to know (a) how a student's knowledge and skills at a particular time compare with an earlier stage in the program or course and (b) how the student's cognitive skills and knowledge—and perhaps noncognitive development—are related to specific educational goals of the teacher, school, or state.

To get such information, a teacher usually tailor-makes tests based upon specific purposes, content, skills, and affective elements of the student's immediate experiences in that class. In this sense, the teacher is creating a criterion-referenced test. Each item in the test probably is related directly, or referenced to, specific aspects of the content or skills taught in a preceding block of experiences or time. The criteria the teacher is likely to use to judge the student's performance will be based on the degree to which specific goals are reached. The standard might be the student's previous performance or a comparison with the performance of other students in the class. For these purposes of evaluation, the national norms of norm-referenced tests would be irrelevant.

A fifth trend that should be reassuring to English teachers indicates that many states have replaced conventional standardized norm-referenced measures with criterion-referenced tests, some states are in the process of doing so, and others are using criterion-referenced tests to supplement norm-referenced ones. For example, Alaska reported to ETS that all tests are "being tailor-made for Alaskan students" and that all tests will be criterion-referenced; Arizona reported that it is planning to shift from norm-referenced tests to criterion-referenced ones; and Colorado states that "all cognitive tests are criterion-referenced measures." Several other states indicated that they have adopted criterion-referenced tests or are in the process of so doing.

The preceding discussion has been an attempt to identify the discernible trends in statewide assessment programs. Such trends may ease some teachers' concerns about the uses of standardized tests and about the future prospects of accountability. Understandably, many teachers do object to the uses of standardized English tests as a means of holding them and their schools accountable to outside agencies and to the public. Some are suspicious of the motives of those responsible for programs of testing and accountability, especially when results are to be fed into a state planning-programming-budgeting system (PPBS) and then become a factor in the allocation of funds. Many feel pressured by these measures and the concomitant requirement that they reduce educational purposes to quantifiable behavioral terms.

In New York City, however, some teachers felt that the accountability plan would provide them with protection against unfair charges about the effectiveness of their teaching. In September 1974, the New York City Public Schools began to administer, in two or three selected schools in each of the city's thirty-two decentralized community school districts plus certain high schools, a "pioneering" system of measuring the effectiveness of these schools. The system had been developed over a three-year period under a contract between the city schools and ETS. According to school Chancellor Irving Anker, as reported in *The New York Times* (April 9, 1974), this system of school accountability ultimately will be administered in the city's 950 schools, attended by 1,100,000 pupils. Mr. Anker said also that the system "will make it possible to compare the performance of schools that are operating under comparable conditions."

Such a project of accountability resulted, according to *The New York Times* (July 6, 1974), from a "provision in the 1969 contract between the Board of Education and the United Federation of Teachers. The union had insisted on the provision, according to the U.F.T., 'as a protection for teachers.' " Further evidence of the U.F.T.'s attitude toward city-wide testing is given in a then current issue of the union's newspaper, *The New York Teachers.* Sandra Feldman, director of the U.F.T. staff, stated that the plan of accountability to be introduced in September 1974, would help teachers "because it is going to help us identify our own effectiveness and give us the concrete proof we need that schools and teachers can do a job if resources are provided." The plan would help "examine all of the factors that affect learning: separate out the socio-economic effects on which the schools have no influence at all; and find out what in-school factors make for effective learning, what works and what doesn't." She reiterated this favorable attitude during the 1974 N.E.A. convention in Chicago. According to that same *New York Times* report, Feldman explained that city teachers participated at the outset in the planning of the accountability program. She said, "We thought we ought to get in and have a voice right at the beginning. Otherwise legislatures and school boards try to impose Neanderthal plans on teachers. When we started the planning, most of the other groups were licking their chops saying, 'now we can get the teachers.' They couldn't understand why we had agreed to help develop an accountability plan." Such supportive statements by a union official may be of special interest to those teachers who are opposed to the very nature of mass testing and assessment and skeptical of the motives of those responsible for these inquiries and of their uses of results.

Perhaps some or none of the trends mentioned in this brief review of recent developments in statewide programs entirely meet reservations many English teachers have about the nature and uses of standardized tests. The teachers may not feel, as apparently do members of the New York City U.F.T., that results of tests actually may be a protection for them or that increased resources may be allocated to schools and districts as a result of the identification, through tests, of greater needs. It is hoped, nevertheless, that teachers will give some consideration to recent developments.

The ETS 1973 assessment report draws upon some of Henry S. Dyer's statements in support of statewide assessment:

> Dyer (1966) reminds us how loudly the critics shouted in response to the plan of a National Assessment of Educational Progress. Some of the arguments raised against National Assessment were: (1) the tests would put undue pressure upon students; (2) the findings would lead to unfair comparisons; (3) teachers would teach for the tests to the neglect of important educational objectives; (4) the program would ultimately force conformity and impose federal control of schools.

> Dyer reacts by stating that "... one would suppose that to assess the educational enterprise by measuring the quality of its product is an egregious form of academic subversion" (1966, p. 69). Dyer sees the need of statewide testing programs for two reasons: continuity in the educational process and stability in educational systems. *State-wide testing can help to bring greater continuity into the educational process if it can bring to teachers a continuous flow of information about the developmental needs of students regardless of where they are or where they have been if tests are seen not so much as devices for selection or classification, but as instruments for providing continuous feedback indispensable to the teaching-learning process.* [15]

As readers examine the characteristics of standardized tests in English and the recommendations and criteria for selecting and using them, all might be considered again within the context of prospects suggested by what appear to be encouraging trends in statewide programs in testing and assessment.

## Problems in Statewide Programs

Encouraging though some trends in programs of statewide testing may be, serious problems remain.

1. One difficulty is the possibility of construing state programs as threats to the local control of schools. According to the ETS testing survey, policies are determined by state boards of education, other state education agencies, and the chief state school officer. Almost all funds come from state and federal sources. In most states, tests are selected by state education agencies and results are reported to state agencies. In some states, these data are absorbed into the planning-programming-budgeting system and may become a factor in decisions affecting the allocation of funds to districts. For example, according to the Iowa report (*Assessment Programs*, p. 32), their Needs Assessment Program will indirectly "provide information for a planning-programming-budgeting system." The New York State report includes recommendations from the Fleischman Commission that made a two-year study of statewide "cost, quality and financing of education." One recommendation is that "school achievement accountability be coupled with fiscal accountability in standardized budgeting and auditing procedures; this system would be established by the Education Department. The achievement and fiscal accountability would have as a basic link the statewide comprehensive information systems to provide facts for long-range planning evaluation and enforcement of state mandates."[16] Such authority and procedures cause uneasiness among school personnel and lay citizens concerned about protecting the principle of community control of schools.

2. Another problem arises from the expressed purpose of using subject-matter test results to evaluate instruction, programs, and educational planning—the goals most frequently reported by the states in the ETS assessment survey of 1973. Teachers are likely to object to any use of results of, say, a single standardized measure that includes aspects of English grammar as a means of judging the effectiveness of an individual English teacher, of all English teachers in a school or district, or of a total English program. This misapplied use of results of a test of a limited scope is for teachers probably the most threatening single feature of testing programs. Consider, for instance, the headline of the previously cited *New York Times* report of the N.E.A. convention: "Accountability Plan Angers Teachers, With Many Foreseeing Threat to Job." The existence of this fear is recognized also in the ETS New York State report referred to above. In an "Overview" of the Pupils Evaluation Program (*Assessment Programs*, p. 59), the report states that "a major problem has been the tendency among some groups, lacking technical background, to use the test results in isolation as a measure of the

quality of the educational program."

3. A third problem complicating some testing programs also is associated closely with teachers' uneasiness about being evaluated on the basis of test results. As a consequence of this and other factors to be mentioned later, many teachers have openly expressed negative attitudes toward programs of standardized testing. For example, the report on the Hawaii Statewide Testing Program (*Assessment Programs*, p. 29) reveals that "among the problems presently related to the program are the developing negative attitudes towards all testing, the lack of understanding as to the usefulness of tests by teacher and student and the difficulty in making meaningful interpretations of results at both the legislative and public levels." A number of other states reported problems posed by some teachers' negative attitudes, especially toward the use of norm-referenced and standardized tests and their apprehension about intended uses of results. Some states using both norm-referenced and criterion-referenced tests report that while teachers manifest a negative attitude toward the use of norm-referenced tests, they apparently respond favorably to uses of criterion-referenced measurements.

Teachers of English have been especially outspoken and resistant. For example, in one state that has to comply with a state law requiring testing in English, several prominent teachers of English and specialists in English education were very strongly opposed to statewide testing in English; when the State Department of Education tried to develop its own tests rather than purchase "as is" tests, these teachers refused to cooperate with the Department and with other English teachers who were helping to develop guidelines for the state's own test.

Such negative attitudes, coupled with the teachers' anxieties caused by associating pupils' performances with the rating of teachers, can also subvert the purposes and the administration of tests. For example, in the Oklahoma report (*Assessment Programs*, p. 69), there is the comment about the "tendency for a few teachers to teach for the test." According to *The New York Times* (April 9, 1971), the New York City Board of Education was concerned with this problem as plans were being made to administer the city-wide reading test that spring: "As a result of several known instances of improper coaching for the tests by teachers and allegations of other improprieties, the Board of Education has asked Chancellor Scribner to conduct an investigation into the citywide conduct of reading tests." The problems continue there. In reporting the city's plans to administer the reading tests during the spring of 1974, *The New York*

*Times* (April 2) stated that "special efforts have been made by central school officials to preserve the 'integrity' of the tests in the face of recurring charges of cheating and coaching by some teachers who supposedly want to look good when the scores become public." Dr. Polemeni, the acting director of the city system's Office of Educational Evaluation, said, "Unfortunately, there is a certain amount of understandable anxiety among principals and teachers. They feel they are operating in a fish-bowl environment and that their professional futures could be affected if the pupils' scores are not good."

These examples clearly illustrate the major differences between evaluation and accountability to the public; the erosive effects of some teachers' negative attitudes and misunderstandings; and the serious consequences of failures in communication among all groups involved.

4. A fourth problem emerges from the relation between the content of a specific standardized test in English and the total English program in a class, school, or district. A single measure may be a woefully inadequate means of yielding data to be used as the basis of judging the worth of contributions by a teacher or of an English program involving a wide range of cognitive and affective goals, content, and a variety of relevant experiences. These difficulties become further complicated by the students' experiences in the array of elective courses offered throughout the nation. If a student chooses a wide assortment of electives in literature, dramatics, and independent study and few, if any, in language and composition, then how well is that student likely to perform on a standardized test that is largely a measure of his command of specific aspects of English grammar, usage, punctuation, spelling, capitalization, and composition?

5. A problem related to the preceding is that caused by any significant discrepancy between a teacher's concept of the subject and a concept that underlies a standardized test. Suppose the teacher has a modern, informed, and somewhat flexible point of view toward the nature and acceptable uses of the English language—particularly toward the language a child acquires in the linguistic environment of home and community—and teaches accordingly. Then the student is expected to perform well on an external standardized test reflecting a traditional, restrictive concept of the English language and its usage, an instrument designed presumably to examine a person's knowledge and command of the language. Teachers are disturbed also by discrepancies between their efforts to stimulate students to read and read and read and to respond to literature as an expression of human experiences, and the kinds of external tests on literature

that students have to take. After providing them with enlarging experiences with literature, teachers often have to administer standardized literature tests that draw mainly, if not exclusively, upon students' memorized information about authors and literary selections.

Regrettably, performances on these kinds of tests are intended to be readily measured and quantified. However inadequately these results may represent the total effects of a comprehensive English program upon students, these statistics have the virtue of convenience and accordingly are just the kind of information most likely to be forwarded to state educational agencies and to be publicized in the local community. Upon this kind of reported information, educational authorities, parents, and other lay citizens judge the quality of their teachers and schools.

6. Linguistic concepts represented by items of some standardized tests constitute a crucial problem: that of cultural bias contaminating linguistic items in a test or indeed the whole test. Creating a "culturally free" test may be impossible; but creating a "culturally fair" one may not be. Such a test is particularly essential in any appraisal of a child's language. Pupils throughout our public schools represent, of course, the full range of the diversity of our culture. The languages and dialects children bring from home and community vary accordingly. In 1974, the United States Supreme Court handed down a decision ordering the San Francisco public schools to ensure the teaching of English to almost 2,000 non-English-speaking Chinese children. But the success of efforts to help all children gain increased facility in language depends, in large part, upon teachers' familiarity with languages and dialects, their acceptance of them, and their capacity to capitalize in their teaching upon the rich resources offered by varieties in language. Involved, too, is the matter of what appropriate adaptations will be made in administering any program of testing in English.

Two examples of counteractions taken by administrators in the New York City public schools reported in *The New York Times* (April 9, 1971) illustrate their convictions that standardized reading tests used by the city schools were biased against black and Puerto Rican children and illustrate also the political processes of educational accountability. Rhody A. McCoy, a black, was administrator of the former Ocean Hill-Brownsville demonstration district from 1967-1970. During that time, he refused to permit schools under his jurisdiction to use the reading tests distributed in the city-wide testing program. He considered the tests to be biased and unfair to black children.

In 1971, Alfredo Mathew, Jr., then the city's only Puerto Rican district superintendent, refused to send to the school board headquarters the test papers of 5,000 children in his district who took the reading tests for primary level. He charged that standardized tests "compound the tyranny of testing" and are particularly unfair to pupils deficient in their use of the English language. Those tests prevent some youngsters "from having an opportunity to demonstrate their skills and serve as a self-fulfilling prophecy of failure." He said further:

> Although we strongly believe in educational accountability and maintenance of standards by the central Board of Education, we cannot accept those standardized tests which may not be fair to our children.
>
> Therefore, I am asking for the cooperation of principals, staff and parents to carefully analyze the test items and test formats of particular levels of the Metropolitan Achievement Tests so that we can recommend constructively what should be done with this year's tests.

Standardized tests can be biased not only in content of items and format but also in the way results are used to predict a pupil's academic performance.

Complexities in the treatment of bias in standardized tests are further illustrated by the reactions of Dr. Kenneth B. Clark, black psychologist, educator, and member of the New York State Board of Regents, the state's highest board in establishing policies in education. He objected to the city's contract with the Educational Testing Service; his objections are somewhat the reverse, however, of what might be expected in a case of bias. The test created during that three-year contract was administered in selected schools in the New York City public schools in 1974. As was mentioned earlier, this test was considered by Chancellor Irving Anker to be a pioneering attempt to separate school and nonschool factors affecting a pupil's learning and to compare his or her academic achievements with those of pupils in somewhat similar circumstances.

But, according to *The New York Times* (March 19, 1971), Dr. Clark "assailed" the Board of Education because he disapproved of the concept of accountability held by Dr. Henry S. Dyer, then a vice-president of ETS. He opposed what he considered to be a de-emphasis upon basic skills, overemphasizing "such variables as the background and environment of children." He advocated, instead, the Board's holding teachers and supervisors accountable for pupils' academic achievement. In discounting the importance of taking into account a child's background, Dr. Clark said: "There is no reliable evidence, for example, that the density of population, race, income of parents and so on, in and of themselves, prevent a child from learning to read. There is multiple evidence that children can be taught by effective teachers without regard to children's background."

Complicated though the whole process may be, the search for bias in standardized tests and the effort to create culturally fair tests must continue.

7. The use of standardized tests to meet the public's demands for accounting to the public poses another problem that seems to be especially irksome and distasteful to many English teachers: having to reduce, in their terms, goals and teaching of English to the simplistic level of quantifiable behavioral objectives. English teachers seem to be in the forefront of those teachers who protest against being expected or required to formulate behavioral objectives for their teaching and their pupils' learning, particularly into objectives that can be quantified. Their alarms even increase when results of such measurements are integral to a statewide PPBS, and thereby may become tied to appropriations.

All this notwithstanding, many other teachers of English do not oppose using behavioral objectives. They apparently do not find them incompatible with their concepts of their roles as English teachers. Some analyses on the range of attitudes toward this controversial, complex matter are presented in the following NCTE publications: *On Writing Behavioral Objectives for English* edited by John Maxwell and Anthony Tovatt; *Accountability and the Teaching of English* edited by Henry B. Maloney; and *Systems, Systems Approaches, and the Teacher* by James Hoetker with Robert Fichtenau and Helen L. K. Farr.

8. A final problem to be identified here is related to the practice of comparing standardized test results to so-called "national norms" and then of projecting comparisons into judgments about the quality of teaching. These norms actually are formulated by publishers of the tests and are based upon performances of pupils who took their tests in various grade levels in schools representing some kind of "national sampling." But a problem seems to arise from the public's assumption that the term "national" bestows an aura of official, infallible, universally accepted status upon these norms. As a consequence, when local results are compared to these norms and published, pupils, parents, teachers, school administrators, and lo-

cal newspapers and other media tend to give special attention to the difference. Such inescapable factors as the local learning environment and other implications seem to get neglected in the media and the public sector.

Although these norms are indeed based upon a sort of national sampling, the sampling might have been done several years earlier, not with contemporaries of pupils currently taking the tests. Moreover, the sampling may not have included adequate representations of pupils in inner-city schools or remote communities, or pupils who are culturally different. Furthermore, the tests may be based upon testmakers' giving inadequate attention, if any, to the range of cognitive or learning styles of pupils. As Alfredo Mathew, Jr., said of the Puerto Rican children in his district of the New York City schools, the format of tests may be inappropriate to certain pupils and may deprive them of an opportunity to demonstrate their skills related to the subject matter the test was designed to appraise. So perhaps the reactions of pupils, parents, and other lay citizens to the results of children's performances on standardized tests might be more realistic if they considered those norms to be "publishers' norms," which they actually are. They are not "national" in the sense that they are suited to the diverse backgrounds of pupils represented nationally, nor in the sense that they have been anointed by some public agency, such as the U.S. Office of Education. The semantic as well as the actual differences in such designations may be quite meaningful in local communities.

## An Illustration from Michigan

Some problems arising from conflicting perceptions of the philosophy, design, and performances in statewide programs may be illustrated by some examples from two publications about the accountability plan in one state. One document is a report written by a panel of three outside educators—Ernest R. House, Wendell Rivers, and Daniel L. Stufflebeam—who were under contract to the National Education Association (NEA) and the Michigan Education Association (MEA) to evaluate the Michigan program for educational accountability.[17] The other is a response written by three staff members—C. Philip Kearney, David L. Donovan, and Thomas H. Fisher —of the Michigan Department of Education (MDE).[18]

Early in their response, House, Rivers, and Stufflebeam state that they believe accountability has important roles at all levels of education. They commend Michigan's six-step model of accountability,

and they report finding general approval of the increased use of ob-
jectives-referenced tests.

But they question the wisdom of any state's mandating an almost
"crash" system of accountability that must be put into effect before
specialists in educational research have evolved any relevant standards and procedures. Also questioned is the degree to which the
state's broad educational goals and standards of minimum performance objectives on achievement tests represent the aspirations, cultures, and learning styles of the diverse population throughout the
state, particularly those living in large cities. They are uneasy about
the state's intentions of publishing for parents the state's educational goals, lest these goals and minimum performance standards
unrealistically raise parents' expectations of what their schools are
doing, or can do, to improve the level of their children's educational
achievements.

At the time that they made their inquiry throughout Michigan,
they found little evidence that information gained through the system of accountability actually was being used by the governor, the
legislature, and educational officials as a basis for making educational decisions. Nor did they find much evidence that local communities received significant help in making their educational decisions. They found most educators interviewed were opposed to the
policy of basing the allocated state funds, to some degree, upon test
results.

In the summary of the report they state:

> The Michigan accountability model itself has many good fea-
> tures. It has stimulated public discussion of the goals of education
> and provided direction for state accountability efforts. It has in-
> volved educators throughout the state in efforts to develop objec-
> tives and it has resulted in pilot forms of objectives-referenced
> tests that some teachers have found useful. Overall, the state's ac-
> countability work has created an aura of innovation and change.

On behalf of the Michigan Department of Education, Kearney,
Donovan, and Fisher respond to the outside panel's report. They
commend NEA and MEA for sponsoring the evaluation and report
that the Michigan Department of Education welcomes the recommendations and the help the panel's report has given to focusing
"attention and understanding of what is being attempted to improve
the quality of public education. . . ." They consider each charge and
recommendation made by the panel from the point of view that
"through criticism comes growth, and the departmental staff itself

must be accountable if it is to encourage others to be accountable."
Only a few of their responses will be included here to illustrate problems resulting from differences in points of view and in interpretation of evidence.

Regarding the charge that undue haste characterized the planning and launching of the Michigan plan without waiting for the
benefits of standards yet to be established by educational investiga-
tors, the spokesmen point out that in the absence of any such research and emergent guidelines, the state had decided to "challenge
the unknown and develop knowledge where none existed." They
then ask that if standards do not exist, upon what criteria did the in-
vestigating panel base its judgments? But now masses of information about the statewide accountability program are being rapidly
accumulated and studied, and, admittedly, problems have arisen in
a project the scope of Michigan's.

The two reports differ on many points. For instance, contrary to
the judgments and interpretations of the panel, the Michigan Department of Education believes that the twenty-two statewide goals
have to be general in nature and reports the following:

(a) that objectives in the affective and psychomotor domains have
been developed and are being incorporated in school programs;

(b) that objectives were developed with the help of hundreds of
teachers, specialists in curricula, and administrators;

(c) that each set of objectives was reviewed by a panel of educators, other citizens, students, and the Council of Elementary
and Secondary Education;

(d) that the department makes a "strong plea" that local communities and school districts develop their own special objectives and means of evaluation to supplement the state's minimum objectives—the state is assisting communities in these
projects;

(e) that the department has an on-going evaluation in "nearly
1,100 projects in over 500 school districts";

(f) that although the state believes the effectiveness of teachers
and administrators should be evaluated, this process should
not be carried on in a threatening manner, nor should data
from results of tests "be the sole criterion";

(g) that each year, about 30 workshops are conducted throughout
the state to help local educators;

(h) that the department knows of many instances during 1970-1974 in which information from the accountability program has influenced educational decisions in the legislature, the judiciary, state agencies, and local school districts.

As perceived by the MDE, the main philosophical issue between the basis of the state program and that of the panel's judgment is this:

. . . whether there is a common core of objectives that transcend local district boundaries and which all schools should help students attain. The department's position is that these objectives do in fact exist, that they are identifiable through a rational process, and that the effort is worthwhile.

The following subsidiary issue identified by the department is related to a question raised by the panel:

. . . whether minority children should always be expected to achieve less and, therefore, be tested with a separate test. The department makes the assumption that there is no reason why most children cannot achieve certain minimal skills; therefore, it is appropriate to determine if such skills are being achieved and, if not, the reasons why. To design a minority group test would certainly be possible, but the question is, Should it be done? The staff say no!

The fundamental purpose of the program, especially of the performance-based compensatory education program is "to demonstrate that Michigan's children, regardless of race, family circumstances, or geographical location, can acquire basic school skills for adult survival."

This exchange between the NEA-MEA panel and the Michigan Department of Education is instructive indeed. The department commends the panel for helping increase the attention given to the state's accountability program. Concerned educators and other citizens elsewhere should also thank the authors of the two reports for focusing what otherwise may be diffuse attention upon some central issues, upon evidence and progress, and upon the need for holding accountability systems accountable. The debate illustrates complexities inevitably resulting from extensive programs venturing into new educational territories. Undoubtedly, other states will also be evaluating their programs. English teachers should get involved in the process or at least keep well informed on such developments.

## Notes

1. Center for Statewide Educational Assessment and the ERIC Clearinghouse on Tests, Measurement and Evaluation at Educational Testing Service in collaboration with Education Commission of the States, *State Educational Assessment Programs, 1973 Revision* (Princeton, N.J.: Educational Testing Service, 1973), p. 1.

2. Educational Resources Information Center Clearinghouse on Tests, Measurement and Evaluation and Office of Field Surveys at Educational Testing Service in collaboration with Conference of Directors of State Testing Programs, *State Testing Programs, 1973 Revision* (Princeton, N.J.: Educational Testing Service, 1973), p. 1.

3. Henry M. Levin, "A Conceptual Framework for Accountability in Education," *School Review* 82, no. 3 (May 1974): 363-391. Levin presents an informative analysis of each of these concepts and of some implications of schools' being accountable to the entire range of their constituencies for "proximate" and "ultimate" educational goals.

4. Frederick McDonald, "Accountability Design Stresses Positive Aspects," *ETS Developments* 20, no. 3 (Summer 1973), presents more information about this point of view and about a model of an accountability system proposed for the New York City public schools.

5. Henry S. Dyer, "The State Assessment Survey." Paper delivered to the Association of American Publishers, Washington, D.C., April 29, 1971 (mimeographed).

6. *Assessment Programs*, p. 69.

7. Garlie A. Forehand, "Evaluation, Decision-Making, and Accountability," in *Accountability and the Teaching of English*, ed. Henry B. Maloney (Urbana, Ill.: National Council of Teachers of English, 1972), pp. 23-33. Emphasis added.

8. *Assessment Programs*, p. 7.

9. *Testing Programs*, p. 7.

10. *Assessment Programs*, p. 7.

11. R. E. Stake, "School Accountability Laws," *The Journal of Educational Evaluation* 4, no. 1 (February 1973): 1-3, as quoted in *Assessment Programs*, p. 7. Emphasis added.

12. *Assessment Programs*, pp. 10-11.

13. *Testing Programs*, p. 5.

14. *Testing Programs*, p. 7.

15. Henry S. Dyer, "The Functions of Testing—Old and New," in *Testing Responsibilities and Opportunities of State Education Agencies* (Albany, N.Y.: New York State Education Department, 1966), pp. 63-79, as quoted in *Assessment Programs*, p. 7. Emphasis added.

16. *Assessment Programs*, p. 58.

17. Ernest R. House, Wendell Rivers, and Daniel L. Stufflebeam, "An Assessment of the Michigan Accountability System," *Phi Delta Kappan* 55, no. 10 (June 1974): 663-669. The full report may be obtained from the National Education Association or the Michigan Education Association.

18. C. Philip Kearney, David L. Donovan, and Thomas H. Fisher, "In Defense of Michigan's Accountability Program," *Phi Delta Kappan* 56, no. 1 (September 1974): 14-19. "This article is drawn from a 35-page booklet titled *A Staff Response to the Report: An Assessment of the Michigan Accountability System.*"

2

# Language Development and Its Evaluation

*Walter Loban*

Power over language is not some sudden burst, like a Fourth of July skyrocket; rather it is like a plant growing and interacting with its environment. Teachers have an interest in knowing whether or not their pupils are advancing at a reasonable rate in command of language, and whether or not ways to demonstrate that growth can be determined through the use of published tests.

Such an interest requires that the main features of effective language behavior first be identified and then evaluated. These main features are concerned with power in oral language even more than with reading and writing, for the living language is the spoken language. Yet, no published test attempts to appraise the spoken word, although a few do seek to evaluate listening. Thus, at the very outset, one needs to be cautious about tests for language growth.

If the central concern, spoken language, is missing, what remains to interest schools in these published tests? The question is of enormous importance, for tests do influence the curriculum, and if they deal with peripheral rather than central language concerns, the taxpayer's money is wasted upon misdirected teaching time and upon materials purchased to further minor objectives.

To reduce power over language to such mechanics of written language as spelling, punctuation, and capitalization is a dangerous oversimplification. These are *not* the true fundamentals of language. The people of this nation need instruction that focuses not only upon details but also upon larger adaptations, such as vigor of thought and precise expression of thought and feeling. A perspective that begins with errors of mechanics rather than with a more complete picture of desirable accomplishment seldom reaches to the really important aspects of language ability—interest, pleasure in doing or using, organization, purpose, and other crucial integrating and dynamic patterns of performance. To be sure, punctuation has its

45

limited importance but it is not as important as having something to say or purposeful organization.

With this in mind, the language development tests were examined for the help they might offer in assessing such matters as the use of language (a) to put order into experience and (b) for clarifying thought, feeling, and volition by making distinctions, modifying ideas, and controlling unity through arrangement and emphasis. The possibility that paper and pencil tests can show much about such aspects of language is not very great, but can they make *any* contribution?

Searching among published tests for any which might help to chart the development of language ability is a disheartening task. Condemnation is easy but scarcely a positive action. We need to ask what should be evaluated in language development and how it should be evaluated. In the interest of better language instruction—for what is taught in the schools shrinks inevitably to what is tested or evaluated—let us try to answer these questions as best we can.

At the heart of the matter, in this reviewer's opinion, is the relation between the schools and the society that shapes them. Is it not possible that in a democracy, state educational agencies could assist schools by identifying and clarifying the goals of instruction in language, sifting what is significant and crucial from what is contributing and subordinate? This assistance would bring into focus the relation language bears to personal and mental development. Instead of administering statewide tests of extremely limited coverage, the state could urge or require its schools to evaluate the significant goals that have been identified and suggest feasible methods of doing so. In monitoring evaluation, the state might encounter districts in which the evaluation was, for one reason or another, inadequate. In such cases, the state could suggest improvements or the model of some other school district.

Emphasis on oral language development is essential to any reformed curriculum. An important reason for its present neglect is the complete absence of oral language in all language testing, whether it be college entrance examinations or elementary school testing. Yet, oral language, by its very nature, cannot be reduced to paper and pencil tests, nor do we know of any variables, amenable to paper and pencil testing, which correlate with oral language power. Even so, if precision cannot be achieved, evaluation is crucial. Without it, the curriculum will continue to neglect this basis for reading, writing, and appreciation of literature and they, in turn, will suffer.

With the development of tape recorders, video tape, and cassettes, the drawbacks to evaluating oral language have diminished. The objections that taping requires too much time and money can be solved easily by using sampling procedures. It is not necessary to record every pupil. In a class of thirty, a random sample of six pupils can demonstrate growth if the sampling occurs in September, February, and May (individual pupils with special or severe problems can be recorded and studied more intensively). Class or group discussions can be recorded in similar situations at the opening and closing of a semester or a year, and from one school year to the next.

Rating scales can be used to identify and check the kinds of items already discussed. Reliability and validity can be increased by adding to the number of raters and by having the ratings carried-out by persons, other than the teacher, who do not know the pupils. The expense of employing such raters would be much less than the money now expended upon published standardized tests.

The development of language power is infinitely more comprehensive and complex than any available standardized test indicates. For this reason, this reviewer cannot in professional good conscience recommend *any* available standardized test as a valid measure of children's linguistic ability.

Insofar as valid tests can be constructed at all, test creators will need to consider the goals described below in any serious evaluation of children's ability to gain power in language. Inasmuch as the living language is the spoken language, most of the abilities listed below should, if firmly developed, contribute also to power over the written language as well as to reading and listing.

Usage that does not distract the attention of the listener. Dialects and various levels of formality may be appropriate, depending upon the situation.

Clear enunciation and articulation.

An ability to cleave to the point without too much qualification, modification, and random associations. This is true for conversations, group discussions, and individual speeches before the class.

Clarity or organization, ability to develop one idea at a time, precision in the use of language, wealth of vocabulary—these assume new importance when the effect upon others is the basic criterion of successful expression.

Ability to get to the point; cleaving to the heart of the matter in discussion, panels, and group work.

Improvement in ability to stick to the point. Do pupils make progress in discussing a point? Are their illustrations pertinent to the concept under discussion?

Are pupils aware of the levels of formality in language? Do they know when to use slang, colloquial, informal, and formal usage? Do they adapt their language to the occasion?

Are they able to use a standard language appropriate to the situation: not offensive, not distracting from the idea. (Examples of nonstandard usage: I seen it; Her and me had a quarrel; I ain't got none of them there new shirts.) Are they learning *why* they should avoid profanity, stale slang, delicate subjects, libel, and smear words?

Are they better able in conversation and group discussion to
   a. make distinctions?
   b. modify ideas?
   c. control unity and coherence through transitions and arrangement?
   d. do they use emphasis to full effectiveness?

A moderation in speed of speech—neither too slow nor too rapid; variation in rate and volume, appropriate to content.

Vitality—involvement; energy of speech.

Effective clustering of words and phrases—and pauses (clustering that contributes to the meaning).

A resonant voice, varied in pitch; characterized by an imparting tone; emphasis (stressing of words) helpful to the listener.

Are the participants on panels and those who give oral reports effectively adapting their manner and presentation to their audience?

Are they using an *imparting tone* and appropriate gestures?

Are primary school children learning to adjust their voices (volume, intonation) to their hearers? (Also their behavior, such as looking at hearers?)

Are pupils learning to adapt their rate of speech to the situation and the ability of their listeners to follow their ideas?

Drama is frequently used to foster growth in oral language. Through it

    a. pupils extend the range, fluency, and effectiveness of their speech,

    b. words move from a passive recognition vocabulary into active use,

    c. words are increasingly used with meaningful intonation.

Awareness of the patterns of sound linked to thought will manifest itself in

    a. sensitivity to standard usage,

    b. concern that others will receive one's communication without distraction,

    c. a distaste for sloppiness and, therefore, distaste for whatever violates grammatical concord.

The pupil must become aware of important rhetorical goals:

    a. the strategies of emphasis,

    b. the skills of exemplifying and generalizing,

    c. the importance of unity and relevancy, gained through imposing order and structure that are dynamic, not mechanical.

A sincerity that enables the words to flow more easily.

Poise from inner security and confidence.

A stable personality, free from timidity, self-depreciation, contentiousness, egocentrism, and all such traits that reveal themselves in speech or manner.

Developing respect for diversity of opinion. Are they learning to welcome differences of opinion because such differences motivate thought? Are they learning to differ without rancor?

Are class discussions showing improvement in courtesy, mutual respect, and thoughtful attention to the feelings and dignity of everyone in the class?

Are pupils gaining the skill to retreat gracefully from an untenable position and to modify their ideas in the light of new evidence?

Do students feel a duty and obligation to express their point of view, even when it is unpopular, so that through democratic process, the group has access to all sides of an issue?

Do students speak without self-consciousness to students of other racial, ethnic, cultural groups? Other socio-economic levels?

Are the very talkative pupils discovering terminal facilities for speech? Are the quiet and laconic pupils using more and better language?

Are all the pupils learning to use language to put others at ease, cheer them up, or draw out their ideas?

Are they learning to discard rigid dogmatic statements and replace them with a "positive tentativeness"?

Are the students gaining in personal poise and self-reliance?

Are students showing any signs of asking for authority and of judging the courses from which they get their information? Do students recognize when statements are backed by opinion rather than fact, and do they feel an obligation to cite sources and facts when these are pertinent?

Informal business meeting procedures and parliamentary procedures enabling pupils to

a. get things done by handling one thing at a time?
b. give the minority a hearing?
c. see that the majority opinion prevails?

Are they learning to detect basic assumptions? The difference between significant and insignificant knowledge?

Are they learning techniques of group discussion and efficient use of time?

Is there wide participation in class discussions?

Do they show a concern for truth in language; do they know why perjury is such a serious crime and so carefully watched in courts?

In addition to the above goals, test creators should consider the findings of research. Research shows that certain language behaviors characterize growth and command. The pupils use fewer short oral utterances; express tentativeness more frequently through statement of supposition, condition, or concession; use more analogies and generalizations; and excel in coherence because they use effective subordination of all kinds—nonfinite verb phrases, prepositional phrases, absolute constructions and appositives, as well as adjective clusters and dependent clauses.

Not grammatical sentence pattern but what is done to achieve greater flexibility and modification of ideas within these patterns proves to be the real measure of proficiency with language. Growth in this attribute is important.

Expression can be improved. Dexterity with oral language can be advanced by identifying the elements of language which strengthen or weaken communication, that increase or lower precision of thought, that clarify or blur meaning. Many of these elements would be such matters as liveliness and energy of speech; sticking to the point; reducing the mazes or language tangles that so often result from too much qualifying, timidity, insecurity, or failure to realize how the listener reacts to so much hesitation.

Increased attention needs to be focused on oral language, not just talk and chatter, but rather on what might be called thinking on one's feet, i.e., learning to organize or pyramid ideas; to cleave to the heart of a topic; to make progress with ideas; to generalize when enough illustrations have been given; and to illustrate when generalizations are complex or new to listeners.

Teachers can help pupils to compare, contract, categorize, and impose structure on loose material. Teachers can also help pupils to use analogy; become more proficient in synthesis by showing how things go together; use induction from particulars to generalizations; use analysis showing how to take ideas apart; use deduction from concepts to particulars.

Pupils and teachers need to be concerned with the good organization of ideas and good coherent thinking; having something to say and organizing it in terms of a purpose; the ability to grapple with expressing one's own ideas or receiving ideas one wants to hear; finding appropriate words to clarify and organize thinking about experiences, feelings, and thoughts; a greater facility with language that emerges because one is forced to use language in widely varying situations.

All of these goals, other than those directly concerned with acquiring and using standard English, are relevant to speakers of social-class dialects also.

# Elementary School Language Tests

*William A. Jenkins*

This introduction is an inductive statement growing out of specific reactions to the tests reviewed and presents conclusions which should have relevance for all who wish to choose language tests for use in the elementary school.

It seems very clear that the authors and publishers of language tests do not recognize the limitation of paper and pencil tests in measuring language arts abilities. Some abilities, recognized as important by every teacher, simply do not lend themselves to paper and pencil tests. These abilities are often thought of as residing in the affective domain, or are called higher-level abstractions or higher-level learnings. However they are defined, they are ignored by the authors and publishers presenting tests which purport to measure all that is important about the language arts and in language arts abilities and skills. Any analysis, even one as perfunctory as some of those made here, shows quite certainly that the tests do not do this.

It is also clear to this reviewer that the manuals which accompany the tests are overcharted and overgraphed. This reviewer concluded that the technical analyses and statistics do add to the mystique of test-making and test-writing, but their educational value must be questioned. Aside from providing information for statistical experts, other test writers, and school administrators who need statistical evidence to back up their claims about the quality of education in their schools, they are of little use. Actually, they tend to clutter up the teacher's work.

This reviewer also felt that test writers oversimplify language in their desire and attempts to reduce it to the relatively mechanical operation of taking a standardized test. Moreover, because of their inability to measure the more complex language elements, this oversimplification is a distortion.

A broader context is needed to measure language arts abilities than it is possible to give in most of these tests. Situational analyses, where the skills actually function, appear to be what is required. Such situations could get at the pupil's ability to organize his or her thoughts, to relate ideas to each other, to distinguish between ideas, to create word thoughts and pictures, and to recognize the difference between using oral and written language.

Without a doubt, standard English is the primary, if not the only dialect recognized by the test writers represented in the tests reviewed here. These writers recognized few, if any, dialectal differences and deviations.

All of the tests reviewed are strong in measuring selected items of achievement, but are just as weak as diagnostic instruments. Lest I be misunderstood, with one or two exceptions they were labelled achievement tests, but in this reviewer's mind measuring achievement is far less useful and perhaps less valid than analyzing children's areas of weakness in some depth so that they may be taught better. The test writers represented here apparently would like to palm off the notion that recognizing an error in spelling, capitalization, or punctuation in an exercise is the same thing as having the ability to use language correctly. This is not the case, and most alert educators know it.

People such as Paul Diederich of the Educational Testing Service have discovered some unusual things about tests. Diederich points out, for example, that, in measuring growth in achievement, students with the lowest initial scores gain most on post-tests, while those in the middle gain less; those with the highest initial test scores gain little or even regress when taking the post-test. Whether tests measure appreciation, attitude, or insight into human relations, or whether they measure knowledge of any sort, these results are the same.

It has also been found that when a teacher gives a published test that measures almost any skill that develops more or less continuously—such as learning to read, write, or do arithmetic—at the beginning of the school year and a parallel form of the same test at the end of the year, the average score is practically certain to rise. Diederich says that the results are influenced by what is known as the ceiling effect, by regression, and by unequal units of measurement, that is, the difficulty in making a gain from 80 to 85 percent is many times harder than from 30 to 60 percent.[1]

These findings raise some interesting questions. For example, if school administrators know that the poorest scoring children will do better on a post-test than on a pre-test, why should they bother to give the pre-test? With *no* instruction, the post-tests will give higher results than the pre-tests. By the same token, perhaps the school administrator should not allow the brightest children to take a post-test because they may regress and show the school in a bad light! Students in the middle group probably should be treated as those in the middle are usually treated—that is, be ignored—because the test results will show that the children have neither progressed nor regressed and thus will neither help nor hurt the school.

It is frequently claimed that one of the reasons for testing students is that taking a test is an experience which reinforces learning. But according to Balch,[2] the opportunity to learn frequently is lost, learning principles are violated, and the potential learning is destroyed. Balch says that learning is always affected both by external elements in the situation, including the amount, organization, complexity, and meaningfulness of the material to be learned, and by internal factors which are characteristic of the learner. One wonders again how a testing situation can be standardized, although test after test claims that it can be, when we have just pointed to five variables that must be taken into account and which certainly cannot be standardized from one testing situation to another. The results absolutely must vary, according to Balch.

All of the above limitations and characteristics of tests perhaps are overshadowed by a condition which appears to make most of the tests reviewed in this section inappropriate for 90 percent of the children in our society: the tests are all written in standard English, ignoring practically every other major dialect. Let us look at this phenomenon. The student most disadvantaged by these tests is the black child. To the majority of black children, being black is almost synonymous with being poor. It is this poverty which prevents many of them from having the kinds of experiences that support the instructional programs of the schools. They are too poor to take trips to cultural facilities. They are too poor to have books and educational toys in their homes. They are too poor to enjoy all of the objects and services commonly a part of the experiential background of the middle-class Caucasian child. They cannot satisfy their educational needs outside of the school. All of these cost money and most black families cannot afford them.

Dr. Kenneth Johnson, a black educator and linguist, points out that to the black child membership in that minority group increases the chances of being culturally disadvantaged.

Culture can be defined as a way of life, a design for living, that consists of the attitudes, beliefs, practices, patterns of behavior, and institutions that a group has developed in response to partic-cular conditions in order to survive. In this country the conditions that existed for the majority of the people have produced the response labelled, "the dominant culture." Black people, however, have had to respond to a different set of conditions, and they have developed a sub-culture that is different in many ways from the dominant culture. . . .[3]

Dr. Johnson goes on to say:

Membership in the black sub-culture contributes to cultural deprivation because it prevents black children from acquiring the middle-class cultural patterns by which almost all school curric-ula and instructional materials are based. Many black children have not acquired from their sub-culture the language patterns, the value system, the attitudes and beliefs—the entire experiential background—that the school program demands. . . .[4]

Probably the most pervasive effect of being a minority group member, coming from a minority subculture, and being raised amid poverty is that the individual child develops a value system which often is radically different from that of the majority. For example, learning and school have negative valences rather than the tradition-al positive ones for minority children. This is explained, in part, by the fact that the child's environment is the negative one of large-city ghettoes. Such an environment restricts the experiences of these children, and the concepts their experiences yield are not those on which the school program is based. To go further, it can be pointed out that children living in a noisy ghetto under crowded conditions and surrounded by much activity are bombarded with stimuli. But they learn to shut out these stimuli in order to have peace of mind. This habit, it is said, becomes a hindrance to them in school because they then shut out the instructional stimuli provided by teachers. Evidence for this claim is the fact that the majority of ghetto children do not have the ability to distinguish meaningful sounds equal to that of the typical suburban child. Another example of a different sort is that ghetto children tend to be aggressive. Because they value aggressiveness over intellectualism, working in groups, one of the chief instructional modes of the school, is antithetical to what they have learned outside of school. Thus ghetto children, and here we are speaking primarily about black children, see few benefits coming from intellectualism as they encounter it in their environment and in many cases are antagonistic toward it.

The disadvantages of black children definitely extend to their language. Because they speak a nonstandard dialect, a number of educators and linguists believe their language interferes with their attempts to read and to speak standard English. They are frequently viewed as being deficient, while in actuality they may be merely different. In their use of language, they are as creative, as intrepid, as effective in communicating as anyone using his or her dialect.

These ideas can be reinforced by pointing to the problems of other minority groups. For example, English proficiency tests which have been prepared for native speakers of Spanish will not be entirely appropriate for native speakers of any other language. As long as one constructs tests that consist mainly of vocabulary, this statement is not a valid one. But for tests which involve more than vocabulary, the statement demands attention when one considers the importance of slight differences in the syntax and phonology of languages revealed by contrastive language analysis.

A different problem might be faced by the Appalachian white child or the ghetto-disadvantaged white child, in contrast to the black child who may suffer because he or she is physically conspicuous. When this condition exists, divergences from the teacher's dialect are likely to be ascribed to innate ignorance. This contrasts with the black child's divergences, which are frequently ascribed to race. As Raven McDavid points out, both ascriptions are equally fallacious.

> The disadvantaged white uses many non-standard grammatical constructions. This is almost tautological, since it is the advantaged who in the long run determine what the grammatical standard is and should be. Where the discrepancy between educated and uneducated speech is greatest, as in the south, the incidence of such non-standard forms will be the highest. The only caution is that there are wide variations in the extent to which the various subcultures tolerate deviations from the norms of formal expository prose.[5]

In summing up all of these differences for the black, for the disadvantaged white, and for the Spanish-speaking child, one must underscore that the teacher avoid forcing an external standard upon students. This reminder is an elementary principle of learning and of language teaching. It is well known that the teacher should simply adapt techniques to the structure of the students' dialect and let the overwhelming power of the culture do its work. However, when one is using a standardized test indelibly written in the language of the major culture, that is in standard English, good teaching becomes impossible and principles of learning are superseded by fairly rigid principles of test giving.

It is a gross oversimplification to say that most of the ills in published tests or in textbooks arise out of the profit-making motives of the publishers and their desire to be publishers for all of the people. But test publishers do have to play down racial, regional, and dialect differences, and have to ignore certain racial and ethnic minorities if their tests are to sell successfully. Just as it is unprofitable for publishers to provide a wide variety of textbooks for the same grade because of the widely differing background of the pupils who will be using them, so it is also uneconomical for publishers to put out a series of tests covering the same grades and ability levels but keyed to the widely divergent cultural, social, economic, and psychological backgrounds of the children to be tested. In the past they mainly have had to ignore these differences and design materials for a general national market. The results may have been economically profitable, but educationally they verge on bankruptcy. The tests, as will be illustrated in the individual reviews, simply do not do what they purport to do, nor what this reviewer thinks they ought to do.

Test publishers, as well as textbook publishers, should base more of what they do upon what goes on in what area, in effect, the several different school systems found in a city: the ghetto schools, the inner-city schools, and the suburban schools. Standardized tests are directed at inner-city and suburban schools, while ghetto schools are usually ignored. Publishers who would consider putting together tests for the latter might examine James Herndon's *The Way It Spozed To Be*, Herbert Kohl and Victor Cruz's *Stuff*, Sylvia Ashton-Warner's *Teacher*, and materials coming out of the Watts Writers Workshop as a first step.

It is clear to this reviewer that the chief deficiency of the tests reviewed is that they tend to ignore the several cultures which make up our society. This deficiency is serious. If education is anything, it is the understanding of and induction into one's own culture, whatever it may be. Unfortunately, these tests evidently measure understanding of only one culture.

## Notes

1. Paul B. Diederich, "Pitfalls in the Measurement of Gains in Achievement," in *Classroom Psychology: Reading in Educational*

*Psychology*, 3rd ed., eds. William C. Morse and G. Max Wingo (Glenview, Ill.: Scott, Foresman and Company, 1971), p. 338.

2. John Balch, "The Influence of the Evaluating Instrument on Student Learning," in *Classroom Psychology*, p. 347.

3. Kenneth R. Johnson, "Blacks," in *Reading for the Disadvantaged: Problems of Linguistically Different Learners*, ed. Thomas D. Horn (New York: Harcourt, Brace Jovanovich, 1970), p. 30.

4. Johnson, "Blacks," p. 30.

5. Raven I. McDavid, "Native Whites," in *Reading for the Disadvantaged*, p. 136.

**New Iowa Spelling Scale.** Harry A. Greene. Iowa City: Bureau of Educational Research and Service, 1954.

**Iowa Spelling Scales.** Ernest J. Ashbaugh. Iowa City: Bureau of Educational Research and Service, n.d.

**Buckingham Extension of the Ayres Spelling Scale.** B. R. Buckingham. Indianapolis: Bobbs-Merrill Co., n.d.


The *Iowa Spelling Scales* (grades 2-8) are lists of words that have been found to be used widely in the written communication of children and adults. The difficulty level in a particular grade is given for each word (a total of 5,507) by the percent of accuracy of spelling for that word in each grade. For example, the word *dandy* is spelled correctly in grades 2-8 thusly: 8, 32, 48, 68, 82, 85, and 88. The scales, then, are not truly tests but rather are a source of material for teacher-made or standardized tests. The scales are still useful, although one has to raise the question whether a scale developed in 1954 is applicable and valid for children in 1976 when one realizes that the chief increase in vocabulary comes in the form of nouns. The things children are interested in have changed considerably in the intervening twenty years.


**Hoyum-Sanders English Test.** Elementary Test I, form B; Test II, forms A and B; Intermediate Test I, forms A and B; and Test II, forms A and B. Vera D. Hoyum and M. W. Sanders. Emporia, Kans.: Bureau of Educational Measurements, 1964.


The Elementary Test I, form B, includes ten sentence recognition questions; fifteen capitalization questions; fifteen punctuation questions; ten contraction, possessive and spelling questions; thirty-five usage questions; and ten alphabetization questions. Test II, form A, and Test II, form B, follow the same pattern.

The Intermediate tests ask ten questions on sentence recognition; twenty questions on capitalization; twenty questions on punctuation; ten questions on contractions, possessives and plurals; fifty questions on usage; and ten questions on alphabetization. Test I, form B, and Test II, forms A and B, follow the same format, although the number of sentences varies slightly.

All questions except the alphabetization, which consists of single words, are posed in the form of sentences or sentence fragments. A context of sorts, therefore, is provided. The test can be hand scored by the teacher. The ease of scoring, plus the ease of administering, have to be considered strengths of the test. Directions, including norms and percentiles, are included in a six-page leaflet.

The authors claim that the purpose of these sets of tests is to measure objectively pupil and class proficiency in the essential *mechanics* of English. The authors also say that the tests may be used for both survey and diagnostic purposes, "They help the teacher determine pupil and class deficiencies and therefore will lead to better teaching." The tests, according to the authors, may be used in a number of ways: (1) for determining pupil achievements; (2) for checking the efficiency of instruction; (3) for assigning school marks; (4) for analyzing pupil and class weaknesses; and (5) for motivating pupil effort.

Compared to other tests, however, these are slim enough to make one question their validity and reliability. On the other hand, the authors point out that the norms were established by administering the test to more than 50,000 pupils in forty-six states. Assuming that the samples used for evaluating pupil performance are valid, the tests may be useful. On the other hand, any test which in today's world stresses mechanics as opposed to the expression of ideas must be considered suspect and of limited use.

**Kansas Elementary and Intermediate Spelling Tests.** Test I, forms A and B; Test II, forms A and B; and comparable forms for Intermediate tests. Connie Moritz and M. W. Sanders (Elementary); Alice Robinson and M. W. Sanders (Intermediate). Emporia, Kans.: Bureau of Educational Measurements, 1964.

Each of the Elementary tests consists of fifty words, each of which has been spelled four different ways; the correct one is to be underlined. The Intermediate test consists of a list of eighty-five words, with four spellings given for each word; the correct word is also to be underlined. Both tests have a time limit of fifteen minutes.

One has to question whether this is really the way to test pupils' knowledge and ability to spell. Recognizing an incorrectly spelled word, it seems to me, calls upon skills different from spelling and writing the word correctly.

The words in the test were selected from the *Buckingham Extension of the Ayres Spelling Scale*, the *Iowa Spelling Scale*, the *Thorndike Word List*, and a number of recognized spelling tests. These publications helped determine difficulty level of the words and the proper grade placement for them. The incorrect spellings themselves were drawn from a study of pupils' spellings and from the incidences of choices of spelling on preliminary editions of the various divisions of the test.

The overall evaluation of the tests has to be made in the form of a question: does the test do anything that a good review test in a speller would not do other than provide norms and percentiles in a manual of directions?

**California Achievement Tests**. Levels 1-3, form A. Ernest W. Tiegs and Willis W. Clark. Monterey, Calif.: California Test Bureau/ McGraw-Hill Book Co., 1970. (See Hook review p. 81 for Levels 4 and 5.)

The *California Achievement Tests* are designed to measure, evaluate, and analyze school achievement from grades 1.5 through grade 12. They are presented in machine-scoreable format. Setting the Mathematics section aside, we find two main sections: Reading and Language. The first, Reading Vocabulary, includes four pictures, one of which should be marked in response to a sentence that is read to the children (ten items); in ten other items children are asked to indicate the first letter of a word that is read aloud; in ten further items children are asked to indicate the final letter of a word that is read aloud. Also under Reading Vocabulary are fifteen items in which children have to match letters; ten items to match words; ten items to match words and pictures; twelve items to match words read with a word heard; and fifteen items to match a word in context with an isolated word. In all cases except one, children are given one of four choices. In the second division, Reading Comprehension, children are asked to answer twenty-four questions based on short reading passages; again, four choices are given.

The second section, Language, covers Auding, Capitalization, Punctuation, Usage and Structure, and Spelling. Auding includes five questions that are read aloud, with the choices to be marked; and ten items in which the children carry out a series of instructions. Capitalization has twenty-four items in the context of a sentence. Punctuation has fourteen items in the context of a sentence. Usage and Structure has twenty items in the context of simple sentences. Spelling has twenty groups of five words, one of which may be spelled wrong.

Among the three different Levels of form A, there are few significant differences from level to level. In Level III there is more emphasis on Usage and Structure, with forty-one items comprising the test. And the brief Auding exercise that appears in Level I is not repeated at other levels.

*Evaluation*

There is nothing particularly distinctive about these tests. Once again, pictures are used in the text. The student has merely to choose the right item from among the three to five presented. Nothing in the tests appears to recognize national, cultural, racial, religious, or socio-economic differences; for example, there is in one picture an amalgamated or homogenized school building, and the same is true for depictions of buses, automobiles, airplanes, etc.

The lack of cultural and socio-economic recognition in the test is probably a weakness. The length of the *Examiner's Manual*, eighty-seven pages for form A, is both a strength and a weakness: for the average classroom teacher, the exhaustive detail may be a liability; for examining departments of school systems, the thorough treatment may be advantageous, if it does not overshadow the test itself. The sections of the test do not appear to be weighted. Therefore, an evaluator must make a comparison between the number of items devoted to specific language skills and consider whether there is a skewness in the test development and whether the number of items adequately reflect knowledge or skill in language use. The sections, from level to level, include approximately the following emphases:

> Reading Vocabulary: 41 items
> Reading Comprehension: 5 items
> Reading in Books: 40 items

Capitalization: 30 items
Punctuation: 36 items
Usage and Structure: 25 items
Spelling: 25 items

Over the years, school administrators and teachers have evidently found this test useful and of high quality. It apparently is an easy test for children to take and for teachers to administer, apart from the very complete *Examiner's Manual*. National norms based on more than 300,000 individuals have been developed for the test and are constantly revised, although the latest edition (1970) simply does not recognize differences in American society. If the samples are valid, English-Language Arts teachers, or at least primary grade teachers, may use the test to diagnose some strengths and weaknesses. The skills measured are basic to a great many learning areas other than Language Arts.

**Comprehensive Tests of Basic Skills (CTBS).** Levels 1 and 2, form Q. Monterey, Calif.: California Test Bureau/McGraw-Hill Book Co., 1968. (See Hook review p. 85 for Levels 3 and 4.)

The *Comprehensive Tests of Basic Skills* is a series of tests with alternate forms for grades 2.6 to 12, divided into four levels that overlap at grades 4, 6, and 8. The batteries test skills in reading, language, arithmetic, and study skills. They can be used for a survey of individual and group performance in basic skills and, according to the publisher, for analysis of learning. They were developed for national use by students who have been taught by different approaches. They generally measure achievement.

In Level 1, the forty-item vocabulary test simply does not seem to be representative of the vocabulary of present-day eight to eleven year olds. In Test 2, Reading Comprehension, the publisher evidently has included items of letter discrimination, word discrimination, and phonics as comprehension. As an example, the student is asked to choose the word from among *knew, keep, basket,* and *book,* in which the *k* does not sound. This is not a test of comprehension. Similarly, the student is asked to mark the word which sounds like *meat,* from among *met, mate, meet,* and *mat.* It should be admitted, however, that most items are not like this. They follow the usual comprehension test pattern of having the student read a paragraph or two and then answer questions on them. The test of Language Expression is satisfactory, as are those on Language Mechanics and Spelling.

The five subtests in Level 2 of interest here are: Test 1, Reading Vocabulary (forty four-choice items); Test 2, Reading Comprehension (forty-five four-choice items based on short reading selections, primarily prose); Tests 3 and 4, Language Mechanics and Language Expression (items in a letter and in an essay which must be filled in with the proper punctuation or capitalization mark for the first twenty-five items and the most appropriate word missing in context must be filled in for the usage items, a total of fifty-five items); Test 5, Spelling (thirty groups of five words each, with one or no words misspelled in each group).

Each of the tests is accompanied by an examiner's manual. The manual describes the test, gives directions for administering them, makes suggestions on scoring, reporting and interpreting the results, and provides norms for the test scores.

## Weaknesses

The weaknesses of the tests have been alluded to in analyses of other tests: the material invariably is in a shallow and minimal context, or not in context at all; little attention has been paid to levels of English usage other than standard English; and the authors have not been much concerned with making the test "culture free," or at least recognizing the widest possible range of cultural contributions to the English language and to American society. The tests are also measures of cognition rather than the ability to perform in the English language arts; that is, students are not asked to speak, write, or listen at all and they do not read for a sustained period. Most measures of ability are taken by inference rather than directly.

## Strengths

The tests can be administered by the average classroom teacher who can get a picture of the relative standing of his or her students, compared with each other, or with classes across the country; and the tests can be administered a part at a time to offset fatigue and to prevent using several entire days of school for administration of the full battery.

**Metropolitan Achievement Tests (MAT).** Primary batteries I and II, Intermediate, and Advanced; forms F, G, and H for each. Walter N. Durost, Harold H. Bixler, J. Wayne Wrightstone, George A. Prescott, and Irving H. Balow. New York: Harcourt Brace Jovanovich, 1970.

**Metropolitan Achievement Tests.** Elementary battery, form A. Harold H. Bixler, Gertrude H. Hildreth, Kenneth W. Lund, and J. Wayne Wrightstone (Walter N. Durost, general editor). New York: Harcourt, Brace & World, 1958.

Test 1 of the Primary I battery (grades 1.5-2.4), Word Knowledge, has thirty-five four-choice words based on a single picture. Test 2, Word Analysis, includes forty four-choice items measuring pupils' knowledge of sound-letter relationships or skill in decoding which are marked in response to an oral question. Test 3 checks understanding of the reading of sentences; three choices are given to describe a picture and the pupil is required to mark the correct sentence. Test 3 also includes the reading of stories of three to seven sentences in length. The pupil is to check the correct description of the story. There are forty-two reading sentences and stories combined.

Five tests in the Elementary battery (grades 3.5-4.9) were examined: Test 1, Word Knowledge; Test 2, Reading; Test 3, Language; and Test 4, Spelling. The test of word knowledge asks the pupil to pick the right word from a series of four which matches a given word. For example, "A husband is a woman, boy, girl, man." The Reading test consists of paragraphs of increasing difficulty which the student must read and answer questions about. A sample paragraph is "Mother made a cake. She put candles on it. The candles told how old I was. Mother got ice cream and candy. She got paper hats. She asked children to come to our house." The questions are (1) "Mother was getting ready for—Halloween, a birthday, Christmas, a picnic"; (2) "What did mother put on the cake? Candles, candy, ice cream, paper hats"; and (3) "The paper hats were to—eat, light, wear, read."

The Elementary Language test comes in two parts; Part A is concerned with usage and Part B is concerned with punctuation and capitalization. Twenty-four usage items are given, the pupil having to indicate whether the usage is "right" or "wrong." In the capitalization and punctuation section, fourteen sentences are given and various parts of the sentence are pointed to. By means of checks or insertion of capital letters or punctuation marks the pupil indicates that the questioned element is right as it is or that it needs changing. In the Spelling test the teacher reads aloud a list of forty words in sentences to the pupils. The word to be spelled is given, the sentence is read, and the word to be spelled is repeated.

The Intermediate battery includes Test 1, Word Knowledge, fifty four-choice items; Test 2, Reading, which includes forty-five questions based on stories which become increasingly longer and more difficult; and Test 3, Language, which has a total of 103 items on usage, parts of speech, punctuation and capitalization, and language study skills. These are all three, four, or five-choice items. Test 4, Spelling, has fifty words in sentence context that must be marked as being spelled correctly or not. The Advanced battery follows the same format as the Intermediate, with the items of greater difficulty.

The test kits include such items as the Individual Profile Chart, Class Analysis Chart, Class Record, Raw Score-Standard Conversion Table, Directions for Scoring, and Directions for Administering. The amount of material to be read by the teacher is indeed great, yet the directions are clear and the test can be administered and interpreted by the classroom teacher.

## Uses for English-Language Arts Teachers

The *MAT* measure, to some degree, what is being taught in the schools, although admittedly most of these items are out of context as far as language arts activities are concerned. The pupil reacts rather than acts. The tests can be administered individually; that is, the Spelling test may be administered at one time and the Vocabulary test at another. As far as certain selected language arts knowledges are concerned, the tests measure achievement, with limited diagnostic uses.

## Weaknesses

The most obvious general weakness of the tests, of course, is that language arts knowledges and skills are taken out of context. It is questionable, for example, whether recognizing a misspelled word and spelling the word correctly when writing call upon the same skills and knowledges. One might also ask whether a single sentence can truly provide a context in which either punctuation or capitalization or usage items can be evaluated. Perhaps a minimum context would be of paragraph length. A second weakness is centered on the question of whether or not punctuation and capitalization are as important as usage, and whether the weighting given to these parts of the test is defensible. A third weakness is that the tests are pegged to the ability to use standard English. Finally, with the exception of the Spelling test, the Elementary battery offers only silent reading tests. They don't get at the oral language of children at all. One cannot assume that performance in oral language will be or can be extrapolated from performance using written language.

### Strengths

The directions for administering the test are complete and clear. The analyses of the test are thorough and thoughtfully done. Provision is made for the performance of individual classes in taking the test, and the various subtests have been divided and analyzed rather well. The test has a good reputation among educators, although it is usually administered by central office personnel rather than by the individual classroom teacher.

### Comment

One is struck by the sameness of tests in the English Language Arts. Although discrete items may vary, the patterns are much the same. Without resorting to statistical analyses of these tests, one finds little difference among them. Thus, one is hard pressed to recommend one test over another.

**Science Research Associates Assessment Survey, Achievement Series**. Blue, Green, and Red Levels, form E. Robert A. Naslund, Louis P. Thorpe, and D. Welty Lefever. Chicago: Science Research Associates, 1971.

The Science Research Associates Achievement Series consists of a set of norm-referenced tests which survey general academic progress. There are two editions in the series, primary and multilevel. The latter is reviewed here.

The multilevel forms—Blue, Green, and Red—are of graduated, overlapping difficulty and are intended to cover grades 4 through 9.

Each set contains tests in reading, mathematics, language arts, social studies, use of resources, and science. Only the Reading, Language Arts, and Sources tests will be reviewed here.

The tests consist of the following items:

| Reading | Blue | Green | Red |
|---|---|---|---|
| Restate Material | 11 | 11 | 15 |
| Sequence and Summarize | 7 | 5 | 6 |
| Draw Inferences | 11 | 14 | 12 |
| Apply to New Situations | 6 | 5 | 6 |
| Logical Relationships | 13 | 13 | 9 |
| *Reading Vocabulary* | | | |
| Phrase Context | 30 | 30 | 30 |
| Story Context | 12 | 12 | 12 |
| *Language Arts: Usage* | | | |
| Capitalization | 11 | 9 | 8 |
| Internal Punctuation | 11 | 13 | 14 |
| External and Special Punctuation | 13 | 13 | 13 |
| Nouns, Verbs, and Pronouns | 19 | 17 | 14 |
| Modifiers and Connectors | 6 | 8 | 11 |
| Linguistic Analysis and Diction | 10 | 10 | 10 |
| *Language Arts: Spelling* | 40 | 40 | 40 |
| *Use of Sources* | | | |
| Dictionary | 10 | 8 | 8 |
| Table of Contents | 10 | 8 | 8 |
| Index | 8 | 8 | 8 |
| References | 12 | 12 | 8 |
| Catalog Cards | No items | 4 | 8 |

The specimen test set included a seventy-six-page booklet, *Using Test Results*, as well as a *Technical Brief* and *Multilevel Examiner's Manual*, far more than the average teacher will need in order to give the tests or will want to know about them. However, the discussion in *Using Test Results* of such things as "Factors Affecting Test Results" and "Communicating Test Results" are good teacher aids. The range of background and exploratory material would aid a school system which is planning a major achievement assessment of its instructional programs, researchers and statisticians who wish to analyze the test development program, and the classroom teacher who administers the test to his or her students. The important question, then, is the reliability and validity of the tests.

The test is based on the premise that there is and should be a relationship between instructional programs and testing programs. Judgments and actions which can affect a school's program can be test-related if program and tests are compatible. But the testmakers hedge a bit—and they should—in pointing out that judgments based strictly on test results which affect individual students should not be taken as sole sources. They should be used along with the teacher's observations and the results from other diagnostic measures.

## Uses for English-Language Arts Teachers

The Reading test measures the ability to understand and evaluate material which the student has read and relate what has been read to other ideas (Comprehension). This is added to a Vocabulary score based on the recognition of common words, usually presented in a phrase context.

The Language Arts test is divided into two sections, Usage and Spelling. Usage measures knowledge—and, to some extent, use—of punctuation, capitalization, manner of expression, word and sentence order, and the organization of ideas. The Spelling test is based on a recognition of spelling errors.

The Use of Sources subtest measures knowledge of the common reference tools and guides: the dictionary, the table of contents, the index, references, and, in the two upper levels, catalog cards.

## Weaknesses

If there is a weakness in these several levels of tests, it must be centered on the limitation of paper and pencil tests to measure all kinds of achievement. For example, the assumption is that if students can choose among several alternative grammatical usage forms, then there will be an indication of their ability to write the language with fluency and accuracy. The test materials suggest, for example, that scores for the Language Arts test indicate the extent of a student's written language skills—how properly he or she can use the English language. This is simply not so. The test will measure speed in making the choices from among language usage items (the tests are all timed) and accuracy in making the right choice. How well the student would compose a paragraph or a sentence or a longer essay cannot be determined and should not be inferred from such a test. The same question might be asked about capitalization and punctuation. Choosing correct answers does not indicate how well a student can capitalize and punctuate written materials. Actually, the test measures the ability to recognize errors and misusages made by other people and, again, to indicate these with some degree of accuracy and speed. Whether the student can write and capitalize and punctuate correctly is still unknown. A transfer from knowledge to use is assumed but not proven.

The same might be said for the Spelling test. The score does not indicate how well a student can spell familiar words. The inference is made that if a student can recognize an incorrectly spelled form or spell a word in isolation as opposed to writing it in context, an indication will be given of the student's ability to spell when writing. This again is a debatable inference.

The claims for the Reading test are more valid. A student's score for the Reading test does indicate the level of some reading skills—how well he or she understands written language and how well he or she can understand the meaning of written words, phrases, or sentences. The score on the Comprehension test tells how well a child can take in information and ideas from stories and essays. The Vocabulary score indicates how well a child understands the meaning of words according to their contexts. The Reading score, then, is a composite score indicating a test-taker's overall achievement level in the test areas at the time of testing.

A moot question, and the most critical one, is whether the knowledge areas in which the child was tested are those that are most critical for effective reading and writing.

*Strengths*

The tests should be as easy to take at grade 4 as at grade 9, although the slow reader who is a good speller might have difficulty in showing it, for this is a silent *reading* test.

Liberal time limits have been set for the tests. However, the overall four and one-half hours (two hours and twenty minutes for the parts reviewed here) can only be viewed as fatiguing.

The interpretive and administrative materials supplied with the tests are bulky but they should be helpful to teachers, as well as to administrators who are planning a testing program and those who are developing comparative data on student achievement. For those educators who read carefully and recognize test limitations, the limitations of these tests are spelled out: the tests measure how much students *know about* certain things and they are best used in comparing one group of students with another. The tests are also reliable. Administration to a sizable number of students and the analysis by a number of education experts have brought them to this level.

## Comment

The authors apparently make no reference to socio-economic or cultural differences among the students who might take the test, nor is recognition given to the fact that urban, suburban, and rural children will bring different educational attainment levels and concepts to the testing situation. Once again, the sameness of all language arts tests is striking. They have been more alike than different for forty years. While the interpretive materials regarding the tests have become more complex and sophisticated, the tests themselves have changed little. We still test spelling ability, for example, on the basis of recognition of incorrect spellings when we give the child a standardized test which must be read. The only major difference among the various tests I have examined, apart from statistical differences, are refinements in wording, in choice of distractors and stems, and the variable weighting given to test sections.

**Cooperative Primary Tests.** Forms 12B and 23B. Princeton, N.J.: Educational Testing Service, 1965.

These tests probe basic understandings of verbal and quantitative concepts at the primary school level. The series includes six tests: Plan-a-test, Listening, Word Analysis, Mathematics, Reading, and Writing Skills. The tests encompass the end of grade 1 through grade 3. The Plan-a-test (ten items) is for practice. The rest are given in this order: Listening, Word Analysis, Mathematics, Reading, and Writing Skills. They attempt to measure major educational objectives regardless of particular curriculum programs and methods. The also attempt to minimize the dependence of one skill upon another and to be as interesting for children as possible. The tests are untimed, although the average time for administration is listed in the testing handbook.

## Uses for English-Language Arts Teachers

It must be emphasized that these tests are primarily for teachers in the primary grades rather than for Language Arts teachers, although they do measure basic understandings supporting advanced work in the Language Arts. The Listening tests (fifty items) are tests of listening comprehension ability. In the main, children simply select a word from three choices that rhymes with, supplements, or is the opposite of the word which the teacher says. The Word Analysis tests (thirty-nine items) measure understanding of structural and phonetic properties of words. By means of rhyming words, analysis of syllables and vowels, initial consonants, ending consonants and so on, this skill is measured. The Reading tests (fifty items) measure the ability to read words, sentences, paragraphs, and longer passages with understanding. After initial instructions are given, the children work on their own. The tests of Writing Skills (forty items), measure the ability to identify correct spelling, punctuation, and English usage.

*Weaknesses*

One cannot help being struck by the sameness of the tests, whether they claim to measure achievement, basic understandings, or basic concepts. I think these are good tests, carefully constructed, with the items chosen with a considerable amount of care. However, except for an occasional unique choice of a word, phrasing, or picture, the tests have little to distinguish them from another dozen or so tests on the market. Perhaps one who would analyze the lengthy test handbook with its forty-one tables and discussion of norming, equating, scaling, and relating would find unique features in the test. But the average classroom teacher will not only not read the handbook, he or she will probably be repulsed by it.

**Tests of Basic Experiences (TOBE).** Levels K and L. Margaret H. Moss. Monterey, Calif.: California Test Bureau/McGraw-Hill Book Co., 1970.

The Language test is one of five tests in TOBE and is available in two forms: Level K, designed for children of preschool or kindergarten age, and Level L, designed for both kindergarten and first-grade children. The test is a measure of the child's mastery of certain concepts which will affect his or her ability to learn further concepts. The test purports to deal with basic language concepts, including vocabulary, sentence structure, verb tense, sound-symbol relationships, and letter recognition. It does so by means of pictures. The child is asked simply to make a straight vertical line to answer a question. For example, a picture is shown of four different items:

strawberries, a carton of milk, a birthday cake, and a carton with a dozen eggs in it. The child is asked to mark the birthday cake by simply drawing a straight vertical line through it. The test includes some nonsense items which get at the child's ability to derive meaning from sentence context. For example, pictures of several items are shown, including a book of matches, and the following statement is read: "The boughs burn. Mark the boughs." The book of matches is, of course, supposed to be marked.

### Uses for English-Language Arts Teachers

The test is really not designed for English-Language Arts teachers. It is more a test for early childhood education where the mastery of basic concepts is more important than considerations of language and vocabulary. Such ability is basic to later Language-Arts work, but it is doubtful that the test should be considered a Language-Arts test.

### Weaknesses

An obvious weakness is whether the items pictured here truly represent the most basic concepts that a child can have. Again, there appears to be no variation for urban, rural, disadvantaged, affluent, urban, and suburban children. Perhaps there should be.

### Strengths

The test is easy to administer and from all appearances should be easy for a child to take. The technical data provided are held to a minimum and instructions are clear. The information on reliability and validity of the test is quite readable. Evidently this is a good test which has been standardized, even if it does not belong within the Language-Arts category.

**Cognitive Abilities Test**. Primary I, form 1; Primary II, form 1. Robert L. Thorndike, Elizabeth Hagan, and Irving Lorge. Boston: Houghton Mifflin Co., 1954-68.

This test is designed to assess the development of cognitive abilities from kindergarten to the first year of college. Primary I, form 1, is for the second half of kindergarten and grade 1; Primary II, form 1, is for grades 2 and 3. However, the publisher recommends a variation in the use of these forms in average communities, communities with high socio-economic levels, and those with low socio-economic levels. The grade placement, therefore, is relative and should be checked on the chart provided with the test.

Both forms consist of a series of five pictures; directions and questions are given orally. The child simply has to fill up a square or mark an oval to answer the questions. The ability to perceive and discriminate is tested, but not the ability to read. Listening is extremely important. The test is presented as a power test, not a speed test; thus, it is not timed. It closely resembles the *Tests of Basic Experiences* written by Margaret H. Moss.

## Uses for English-Language Arts Teachers

The test purports to measure skills basic to learning to read (as well as learning arithmetic and science). The authors claim that a child who obtains a low total score on the test is likely to have considerable difficulty in learning to read and in adjusting to other demands of the formal school situation. It seems to me that this would follow, since the ability to perceive and discriminate are basic to many learning activities. The test is constructed with items ranging from easy to difficult. As a matter of fact, some of the advanced questions in Primary II, form 1, are indeed difficult, and appear to be like questions which appear on the Army classification test and other tests of general intelligence.

## Weaknesses

A potential, though perhaps not real, weakness of the test is whether it can discriminate among youngsters and whether it can achieve its objective of revealing "the full range of individual differences in kindergarten and grade 1." The second possible weakness is whether or not the extreme differences created by socio-economic deprivation and cultural differences have been accounted for. At the time that the test was originally copyrighted in 1954, such considerations were not recognized. There is no evidence that the 1968 revision of the test takes account of this variable. As in tests of this sort, one must always ask whether or not what are truly basic concepts have been included, or whether the sample provided is truly representative. It appears that the effectiveness of the test to no inconsiderable degree resides in the ability of the teacher to read the oral directions, to sustain the children's attention to a task for a fairly lengthy period of time, and to make clear the directions to the test which at times might become a bit difficult. I include this example from Primary II, form 1, to show the difficulty in listening to the test: "Look at the *two boxes* all by themselves. (Pause) Now, find a box that shows how many *more* sticks there are in the *first* box than in the *second* box. (Repeat) Fill in the oval under the box you chose."

## Strengths

The test has been thoughtfully prepared, it should be easy for most children of average ability to understand, and the teacher experienced in administering tests to children should have no difficulty with it. The technical information on scoring and recording how to use the test results, the reliability and validity data, the table of norms, and the percentiles are held to a minimum, and do not overshadow the test itself. The variation for socio-economic level recommended by the authors and the kinesthetic use of the finger to establish the place in the test to prevent the children from becoming confused are also good points.

# Tests on the English Language

*J. N. Hook*

In his introduction to this book, Professor Alfred Grommon quotes a 1971 NCTE resolution that urges the study of "standardized tests of English . . . in order to determine the appropriateness of their content to actual instructional goals and the appropriateness of test norms to students" and the "problems in the use and interpretation of tests." This section is an attempt to re-examine tests of the English language with those madates, particularly the first, in mind.

The tests reviewed here, if the various forms are counted separately, total well over a hundred. Reading the thousands of items contained in them enables the reviewer to draw a few conclusions about the largely unsatisfactory state of the art.

Very noticeable is the narrow coverage of the tests. One finds nothing about dialects. Nothing about history of the language. Almost nothing directly about semantics, unless one counts vocabulary items as semantics. Nothing about etymology. Little, except in a very few tests, about the actual working of the English sentence. All these aspects of the language are becoming of increasing importance in the English curriculum, but the makers of the tests reviewed here have not yet caught up with the profession. Once they are included in tests, such facets of English are likely to attain even more frequent inclusion in courses of study, for tests do influence curriculum.

Still more obvious is the testmakers' concern for "correctness." Some three-fourths of all the items in these tests ask the students to determine whether or not something is "correct": a spelling, a choice of verb, an arrangement of sentence parts, etc. These tests confirm the stereotype of the English teacher as someone primarily interested in catching someone making errors: "Oh, if you're an English teacher, I'd better be careful of what I say."

The urge to measure "correctness" is of course an outgrowth of what English teachers have stressed, and the general public has expected or demanded, for many years. So testmakers should not be blamed for supplying what the buyers have wanted. But the resulting tests, unfortunately, have a built-in cultural bias. Students most likely to do well on them are those from educated, white, Anglo-Saxon homes, who heard "good English" while lying in their baby cribs and have seldom heard anything else. Students less likely to do well come from less-educated families, are often nonwhite, and frequently come from homes where a language other than English is the first or only language spoken. Test results for "correctness," in all fairness, should not be used to make invidious comparisons among students. And if "correctness" is less important than other aspects of language use, such as clarity, directness, and effectiveness, perhaps testmakers should de-emphasize it and try harder to measure what is most important.

Some of the testmakers have simply not kept up with developments in the scholarly study of usage. In consequence, they count as wrong a number of answers that usage reports like those of Margaret Bryant, Bergen and Cornelia Evans, and Raymond D. Crisp show are established, and some (e.g., past tense *sunk* and *sung*) that are included without comment in dictionaries as reputable as *Webster's Third*. Also, in almost none of the tests is social context considered—the fact that a usage not suitable for a very formal paper may be quite satisfactory in ordinary conversation or in a letter to a good friend.

Artificiality of items varies from test to test. Occasionally, the reviewer wonders whether some of the testmakers have ever seen the inside of a classroom or read a composition by a child; some of the sentences they offer for student reaction were not just dreamed up but may have been nightmared up.

Despite protestations in some of the manuals, most of the tests reveal students' ability to recognize but not necessarily their ability to perform. Thus time after time students are asked to identify which one in a group of words is misspelled, but seldom are they asked to spell. Time after time they are asked whether a word is used correctly, but seldom are testmakers ingenious enough to compose test items requiring students to show whether or not they use the word correctly. Scoring ease is usually the villain; a test of student performance rather than of recognition ordinarily takes longer to score and hence is avoided, although a few clever testmakers have gone far to whip this problem.

Review of these tests shows still another serious deficiency: the lack of adequate diagnostic instruments. For instance, though a spelling test may reveal that a given student scores only 70 percent, it does not show what the student's spelling problems are; if it did offer a diagnosis of individual cases, remediation might be easier. Similarly, there should be diagnostic tests that indicate major problems each student has with verbs and pronouns, and with sentence construction. At present, only by time-taking, unguided labor can a teacher find a student's specific areas of weakness, once the test results are available. Something much more specific than just a total score on spelling or on grammer is needed. Testmakers would serve the profession better than they have if they could come up with some good diagnostic instruments instead of concentrating on achievement.

As the reviews indicate, a few favorable comments may be made on a number of the tests. One is that testmakers have largely abandoned the old-fashioned items dealing with mere grammatical identifications: picking out subjects or indirect objects, labelling adjectives and adverbs, identifying complex sentences, and the like. Another is that some testmakers escape several of the criticisms made above, although none escapes entirely. There is at least one test that tries to measure knowledge of how the sentence works; there are a few that require the student to spell a word and not just recognize that it is misspelled; and there are a few that pay considerable attention to sentence effectiveness and not just correctness. Some testmakers have displayed considerable ingenuity in their development of tests that are interesting to take and fairly useful in what they reveal. Improved versions of such tests may be of value in making measurements useful for purposes of accountability.

But there is still far to go before the profession is well served by those who construct tests of the language. Several excellent English language tests or batteries of tests should be available from which teachers may choose in light of the needs of their own students. At present the range is from *very poor* through *poor*, and *fair* to *good but limited*. Still to be reached is *excellent and extensive*.

The reviewer can not assert that the criteria he followed in his evaluation are the only ones possible, or that they are assuredly the best. In any case, the basic criteria followed are these.

1. Study, and therefore testing, of the English language should be broadly conceived to include language history, semantics, dialects, grammar (in the sense of description of the actual arrangements and workings of the English sentence), usage, spelling, punctuation, principles of word choice, and accuracy

and extent of vocabulary. Some borderline areas—spelling, punctuation, word choice—may justifiably be treated in either language or composition tests. In fact, these two areas often overlap. All the branches of English language study listed obviously cannot be included in one test, but language tests taken as a whole should cover them all.

2. Items chosen should be as free of cultural bias as possible.
3. Language use rather than theory should be stressed.
4. Tests should be measurements of students' ability to *do* rather than their ability to *recognize*.
5. Debatable items in spelling, usage, punctuation, etc., should be excluded.
6. Tests should in general reflect the standards of language use that are generally characteristic of the writing found in reputable books and magazines in the second half of the twentieth century; that is, they should be up to date rather than a reflection of the writing of years ago. (Ideally, since language is at base a spoken thing, tests should be no less concerned with the spoken language, but effective pencil and paper tests of spoken language may by definition be impossible.)
7. Results of tests should be usable in planning improvements in a school's language program and in individual evaluation and diagnosis.

**Evaluation and Adjustment Series, Brown-Carlson Listening Comprehension Test.** Forms AM and BM. James I. Brown and G. Robert Carlsen (Walter N. Durost, general editor; Harry A. Greene, coordinator for Language Arts tests). New York: Harcourt, Brace & World, 1953 and 1955.

This test is designed to measure comprehension of the spoken language at high school and college levels. The test-taker is supplied with only a special answer sheet. The administrator reads the seventy-six test items aloud. Time required is "one class period," i.e., about forty minutes.

Part A, Immediate Recall, consists of seventeen items in the form "In the series of numbers 4-5-3-2-1 the *first* number is _____." Part B, Following Directions, tells students to perform twenty simple operations with a set of numerals and letters printed on the answer sheet. Part C, Recognizing Transitions, consists of eight sentences read without context, to be identified as introductory, transitional, or concluding. Part D, Recognizing Word Meanings, requires students to select from a list on the answer sheet the meanings of ten words in context, e.g., "The soldiers *pitched* their tents." And in Part E, Lecture Comprehension, students listen to a twelve-minute "lecture" on vocabulary-building and then answer twenty-one questions concerning both details and main ideas.

*Estimate of Validity and Usefulness*

This is a well-conceived, rather imaginative test that has not been superseded in the many years since it was constructed. None of the test items has become seriously outdated.

One slight weakness is that the test items must be read aloud by the examiner. Some examiners do not enunciate clearly; some will inevitably pause longer than others while the students choose their responses. In consequence, percentile ranks of students, in relation to national norms, may be affected by the examiner. If the test were put on a record or a tape, this problem could be eliminated.

As the manual says, "The mere administration of the test is likely to awaken in students a recognition of the importance of listening skills and an understanding of the fact that people vary greatly in their listening ability just as they do in most other characteristics." Once such understandings exist, students may be motivated to undertake various class and individual projects to improve their listening skills.

**California Achievement Tests (CAT).** Levels 4 and 5, forms A and B for each. Ernest W. Tiegs and Willis W. Clark. Monterey, Calif.: California Test Bureau/McGraw-Hill Book Co., 1970. (See Jenkins review p. 61 for Levels 1-3.)

The *California Achievement Tests* consist of a series of test batteries in five overlapping levels with alternate forms A and B. Only Levels 4 and 5, for junior and senior high school use, are described here. A complete battery consists of tests in reading, mathematics, and language.

The contents of the language tests are as follows:

|  | *Items, Level 4* | *Items, Level 5* |
|---|---|---|
| Mechanics | 72 | 80 |
| Capitalization | 40 (7 min.) | 40 (9 min.) |
| Punctuation | 32 (14 min.) | 40 (16 min.) |
| Usage and Structure | 50 (14 min.) | 54 (14 min.) |
| Spelling | 32 (8 min.) | 32 (8 min.) |
| Totals | 154 (43 min.) | 166 (47 min.) |

Each capitalization test consists of two "stories" and some sentences, divided into lines of no more than five words. A line may or may not contain an error in capitalization. If an error exists in a line, the student is to give the number of the word wrongly printed. The punctuation tests are similar in format; five punctuation marks (period, question mark, exclamation point, apostrophe, and comma) are involved. The first part of each usage and structure test consists of twenty-eight or twenty-nine sentences that may or may not be written in standard English. The student marks T(rue) for Standard and F(alse) for Nonstandard—possibly a trifle confusing. Next come a few sentences concerning transformations, specifically, whether a given sentence can or cannot be transformed into other specified sentences. Then there are six sentences to be classified as complex, compound, simple, or fragmentary. Finally, there are about ten sentences in which some sort of grammatical identification is called for, e.g., the type of pronoun that *somebody* is. Each spelling item consists of four words, with the student indicating which word, if any, is misspelled.

According to the *Test Coordinator's Handbook*, the tests attempt to synthesize traditional, structural, and transformational grammars, so that "the nature of language is really examined."

### Estimate of Validity and Usefulness

As is true of most tests of capitalization and punctuation, this requires recognition rather than doing. A few items are questionable. Journalists write Mississippi *r*iver and some book publishers also prefer *r*iver to *R*iver; the test gives credit only for the capital. For "Wow what an idea!" only a comma is regarded as suitable after *Wow*, so a junior high school student, overlooking the subtle difference created by the small letter in *what*, is penalized if he or she says an exclamation point is acceptable. In neither the capitalization nor the punctuation sections is the matter of unneeded capitals or punctuation taken up. Yet all teachers know that many students capitalize and punctuate excessively.

Some of the usage and structure items may be criticized. Why, for instance, is *everyone* called a personal pronoun in test 5B? Why do these testmakers still beat the *who-whom* horse? If 79 percent of seniors consider an item standard (Usage, 5A, item 29), can testmakers say with assurance that it is nonstandard? Another question (Usage, 4A, item 6) penalizes the student who thinks that *sunk* may be used in standard English as a past tense, but even the conservative *American Heritage Dictionary* says that it may be. Item 18 in the same test implies that *myself* must not be used for *me* as part of a compound object, but the Evans usage dictionary calls the construction "normal spoken English." In 4B, "The boys and they all helped yesterday" is called nonstandard. The sentence is certainly stiff and ugly, and you and I wouldn't say or write it, but what is nonstandard about it?

About an eighth of the items in usage and structure deal specifically with transformational grammar, asking whether a given sentence can be transformed into another given sentence. Those questions are only slightly technical; most can be answered even by students who haven't studied TG. But the ones who have obviously possess a slight edge.

A few more caveats. The answer book says that "Gary and his father like to play pool because it is a game of skill" is a compound sentence. Oh? And what part of speech would you say fits the blank: "The fat pigeon waddled _____ to the curb"? Is it a conjunction, a noun, an adjective, an adverb, or none of these? The answer book says "none of these." But wouldn't a word like *over* or *close* be an adverb here? And students may lose a point if they don't know what a "participle inflectional morpheme ending" is. Only 17 percent of high school seniors guessed right on that one. The law of averages says that 20 percent should.

The words in the spelling tests seem appropriate for the designated grade levels. Students, though, are once more required only to recognize and not to perform.

The supplementary materials for these tests are among the best available anywhere. The tests themselves, despite their problems, are better than most, yet it is too bad that the numerous small flaws were not eliminated. Many thousands of dollars must have been spent on these tests. For just a few dollars more, a couple of English experts could have made the tests considerably better.

**California Short-Form Test of Mental Maturity.** Level 3, S-form. Elizabeth T. Sullivan, Willis W. Clark, and Ernest W. Tiegs. Monterey, Calif.: California Test Bureau/McGraw-Hill Book Co., 1963.

Of the 120 items in this test, twenty-five are in a verbal comprehension (vocabulary) section, in which the test-taker selects synonyms. Also of some interest to a teacher of English is a memory test. For this, a selection is read to the students at the beginning of the test period, and at the end they are asked questions about it. This section, then, tests not only memory but also listening ability. The remaining five sections of the test are nonverbal (three), involving recognition of pictorial opposites, similarities, and analogies; and numerical (two), involving solution of simple arithmetical problems. (Some of the illustrations used in the nonverbal section are rather indistinct.) Total working time for the test is forty-one minutes. A tape recording is available for administration.

Tests on other levels, O (Pre-Primary) through 5 (Adult), are available but were not examined for this report.

*Estimate of Validity and Usefulness*

No attempt is made here to estimate the worth of this test for mental measurement. In the vocabulary section, the words seem of appropriate difficulty for junior high years.

**Clerical Skills Series**. New Rochelle, N.Y.: Martin M. Bruce, 1966.

The English-related tests in the series are Word Fluency, seventy-five partial words, e.g., *Po*_____, to be completed by the test-taker to make any word he or she knows of four letters or more (five minutes); Grammar and Punctuation, forty sentences that may or may not have an error in grammar or punctuation (untimed); Spelling, ninety misspelled words "obtained from typewritten letters," to be spelled correctly (untimed); Vocabulary, fifty multiple-choice items (untimed); and Spelling-Vocabulary, sixty items requiring the test-taker to recognize an incomplete word and spell it correctly, e.g., "DEF____T: win over, vanquish" (untimed).

*Estimate of Validity and Usefulness*

The Word Fluency test is a simple but interesting device that probably reflects quickness of mind at least as much as size of vocabulary. The Grammar and Punctuation test contains a few arguable items: "Data proves" is considered wrong, as are *hung* for *hanged* and "it was me." Only five of the forty items contain errors in punctuation. The Spelling test has the virtue of requiring the test-taker to spell, not just recognize. A few of the words chosen seem a bit odd: Who today is likely to need to spell *fedora*? Misspellings like *seude* and *escalter* may puzzle some test-takers.

Some of the words in the Vocabulary test are unlikely ever to be used again by most test-takers: *shah, treadle, cresset, toucan, doge, defedation, trier,* and *pensile*. In fact, *Webster's Third* labels *defedation* archaic, and "lever," the test's definition for *treadle*, isn't quite satisfactory. The Spelling-Vocabulary test is a simple but ingenious way to check simultaneously on acquaintance with the spelling and the meaning of words of the approximate difficulty of *fl(ig)ment* and *z(ea)lot*.

It is interesting to note that, according to the manual, the Word

Fluency, Vocabulary, and Spelling-Vocabulary tests all have a high correlation with the *Otis Mental Ability Test*.

**College Qualification Tests.** Test V, form A. George K. Bennett, Marjorie G. Bennett, Wimburn L. Wallace, and Alexander G. Wesman. New York: The Psychological Corporation, 1956.

Test V is a fifteen-minute verbal test, one of three parts of a battery intended to be "broadly predictive of college success." The other parts are a numerical test and a wide-ranging information test. The test consists of seventy-five vocabulary items, fifty of which require identification of synonyms and twenty-five, identification of antonyms. Four choices are given for each item.

*Estimate of Validity and Usefulness*

The first half of the synonym section and most of the antonym section consist of words that any reasonably well-read high school senior should know. The remaining twenty-five synonym items are more rarely used words of the approximate difficulty of *voracious* and *eschew*. Median score for college freshman men is 44-45; for college freshman women, 48-49. High school teachers who are interested in finding how their students compare with college freshmen in vocabulary can get a quick approximate answer in this test.

**Comprehensive Tests of Basic Skills (CTBS).** Levels 3 and 4, forms Q and R. Monterey, Calif.: California Test Bureau/McGraw-Hill Book Co., 1968. (See Jenkins review p. 63 for Levels 1 and 2.)

The *CTBS* complete battery consists of ten tests in reading vocabulary, reading comprehension, language mechanics, language expression, spelling, arithmetic (3), and study skills (2). Levels 1 and 2 are for grades 2.6-6; this review concerns Levels 3, grades 6-8, and 4, grades 8-12, only. The publishers claim that "these tests aim to measure . . . those skills common to all curriculums and needed for success in using language and number skills in any school in which the students of our mobile population find themselves."

Items in the language tests are as follows:

Mechanics: twenty-five items (thirteen punctuation, twelve capitalization) based on underlined and numbered portions of a letter and an article; the student indicates whether the punctuation and capitalization are correct or, if not, what the best alternative is. Eleven minutes.

Expression: thirty items (ten usage, ten appropriateness, ten economy and clarity) based on passages of prose and poetry; the student chooses the best alternative among suggested answers. Sixteen minutes.

Spelling: thirty items; the student selects an incorrectly spelled word in a group of four, or observes that none is incorrect. Eight minutes.

## Estimate of Validity and Usefulness

The provision of context for most of the language items in *CTBS* may be helpful. However, there are small but annoying flaws in these contexts: *article* is misspelled *acticle*; the punctuation is incorrect in the line "A hunter, keen and brave, as he"; and the poetry examples are doggerel. In fact, the contextual prose, as well as the poetry, is not well written. And no one except somebody from the Far West would say that the home of the Green Bay Packers is in the East.

Other flaws are also much too numerous. According to Level 4, form Q, "We laugh we cry we learn" should be punctuated with commas, but according to Level 4, form R, "We laugh we cry we live other people's lives a while" should be punctuated with semicolons. The test authors are apparently unaware of restrictive appositives, for they insist on a comma in "the phrase [,] 'Form follows function' " and in "the column [,] 'Shop by Mail.' " In *Brooklyn zoo*, according to the testmakers, *zoo* should be capitalized, despite the fact that newspapers and many magazines would use lower case. In the spelling section, I have no certainty about what word the misspelling *viens* is supposed to represent—possibly *viands*, but that is a much rarer word than most in the test. Also in spelling, how realistic is it in our urbanized society to expect a junior high school student to know about "alphalpha" (alfalfa)? There are still more of such blunders or blemishes, small but indicative of lack of sufficient care.

It seems unfortunate, too, that testmakers who measure skills have so far been unable to find ways of measuring ability to do rather than just to recognize. Presumably one who recognizes a mark, usage, or spelling as right or wrong will also be likely to use the "correct" one in one's own writing. But the presumption does not always prove valid. Every teacher has known students who can do well on recognition tests like these but who make numerous mistakes in their own papers.

In the usage test, the idea of having some items dealing with appropriateness of diction is a good one, as is the idea of having ten items in which the student must choose the most clear and economical of four versions of a part of a sentence. To make room for these kinds of items, the testmakers had to sacrifice some of the usual items, such as *wrote* vs. *written* or *he* vs. *him*. The decision was a wise one.

**Concept Mastery Test.** Form T.  Lewis M. Terman. New York: The Psychological Corporation, 1950.

This test, designed for college upperclassmen and graduate students, is intended as a measure of "ability to deal with abstract ideas at a high level." It has no time limit but ordinarily takes about forty minutes. Its subject matter is derived from "a wide variety of subject matter fields, such as physical and biological sciences, mathematics, history, geography, literature, music, and so forth."

The test has two parts. In the first, the test-taker indicates whether two words are synonyms or antonyms. The difficulty increases, so that near the last of the 115 items the test-taker may encounter words like *sempiternal* and *transilient*, a word not included in three of four desk dictionaries. Part II, Analogies, is in the form "Shoe: Foot:: Glove: (a. Arm b. Elbow c. Hand)" and consists of seventy-five items.

*Estimate of Validity and Usefulness*

Norms given in the manual include scores for the intellectually gifted children studied by Terman from 1921 on; 1004 of them took this test in 1951-52 and had a mean score of 136.7 out of 190, far higher than graduate students in general or electronic engineers and scientists. Air Force captains (344 of them) scored an unbelievably low 60.1.

This is an amusing test for the intellectually minded, but it certainly can also do what is intended: serve as a measure of ability to deal with abstractions, although not all are on a high level. One must remember, of course, that there are other ways to deal with abstractions besides thinking in terms of synonyms, antonyms, and analogies, but those kinds of classification are the most basic.

**Cooperative Academic Ability Test (AAT).** Forms A and B. Princeton, N.J.: Educational Testing Service, 1963.

The *AAT* is comparable in purpose to the *School and College Ability Tests (SCAT)*, the *Scholastic Aptitude Test (SAT)*, and the *American Council on Education Psychological Examination (ACE)*. It is not an intelligence test, but a test that "measures skills in handling certain specific kinds of verbal and mathematical material." It is called a test of power rather than of speed. (Note: the *SCAT* manual says that *SCAT* Series II tests, forms 1A and 1B, were formerly the *Cooperative Academic Ability Test; SCAT,* however, exists on four levels, *AAT* on only one.)

This test consists of two parts, verbal and mathematical, with a total working time of forty minutes. The verbal part (twenty minutes) contains fifty analogies of this type: "tinkle: bells:: A. whistle: tunes B. glide: snakes C. rustle: leaves D. wrinkle: fabrics."

*Estimate of Validity and Usefulness*

As the test manual says, "Verbal analogies have long proved a respectable part of aptitude batteries." They necessarily combine at least a modest command of vocabulary with ability to see relationships. In this test, many of the items consist of simple, tangible things like *water* and *paint*, but other words are of a difficulty approximating that of *dole* or *inimical*. Obviously, the student who does not know *inimical* cannot reason about its analogy with some other word. The analogies represented in the individual test items all appear fair and logical.

The manual says, "The Cooperative Test Division recommends the use of percentile bands in interpreting scores to students. Bands suggest the imprecision characteristic of all such test scores (each band is two standard errors of management wide) and serve as guards against such interpretations as this: Jones's score is 152 and Smith's is 151, so Jones is better than Smith! If two bands overlap . . . one is not justified in concluding that there is any real difference in the two standings. If the two bands do *not* overlap, one is on firmer ground in talking about a difference." Words like these should be printed in large boldface type in every test manual, because testing is still an inexact science and is likely to remain so.

The manual reports a validity coefficient of .52 for the verbal test of *AAT* with regard to class rank of 518 students. This statistic shows a moderately high positive relationship and suggests that the verbal part of *AAT* may be a pretty good predictor of academic achievement.

**Cooperative English Tests, English Expression.** Forms 1A, 1B, 2A, 2B, and 2C. Princeton, N.J.: Educational Testing Service, 1960.

The tests are similar in structure but vary in difficulty. Each test has a fifteen-minute, thirty-item Effectiveness section and a twenty-five-minute, sixty-item Mechanics section. The levels covered are grades 9-14.

The Effectiveness section is largely concerned with vocabulary, but instead of the usual pick-a-synonym variety, this test offers a sentence with one word left out. The test-taker is asked to fill in from a list of four words the one most appropriate to the context. About a third of the items, however, offer four variations of the same sentence; the test-taker chooses the most effective of the four.

The Mechanics section consists of items like this:

> E   When all the marks were
> F   added together, his standing
> G   was fourth in the class.

The test-taker marks *G* on the answer sheet to correspond to the line containing an error (or *O* if there is no error).

*Estimate of Validity and Usefulness*

The Effectiveness section might be improved if there were about an even balance between vocabulary and other items, so that certain sentence problems not illustrated by this test could be included. However, the format of the vocabulary items in this test seems to this reviewer much superior to that of the usual vocabulary test. A student who chooses the most effective word from a group of four obviously not only knows the definition of the word but also recognizes its suitability to a given context; further, the student shows that he or she can distinguish it from three near-synonyms. In two or three instances, though, more than a single choice could be defended.

As is true of most tests on mechanics, this one has some picky or even questionable items, similar to "most every day" and "alright," both of which are here considered unqualifiedly wrong. In general, though, the items are well chosen; their selection was based upon a study of the frequency of student errors. Items in the high school test tend to contain elementary illiteracies like "had went" and "my sister she"; items in the college test are definitely more sophisticated. In the items as a group, there is a good balance of spelling, punctuation, and usage problems.

**Cooperative School and College Ability Tests (SCAT).** Series II: Level 1, forms A, B, and C; Level 2, forms A and B; Level 3, forms A and B; and Level 4, forms A and B. Princeton, N.J.: Educational Testing Service, 1966.

*SCAT* tests are verbal and mathematical, covering grades 4-14. The twenty-minute verbal section of each test consists of fifty analogies of the form, "calf: cow:: A. puppy: dog B. nest: bird C. horse: bull D. shell: turtle." The tests were "designed to provide estimates of basic verbal and mathematical ability," and thus to serve "as a measure of a student's ability to succeed in future academic work."

*Estimate of Validity and Usefulness*

Statistics in the manual show that when comparisons are made between *SCAT* scores and academic performance, the tests "can be useful as predictors of academic success. . . . It should be noted, however, that there is variation in the correlation coefficients obtained at various schools, and when possible schools should conduct their own studies on the usefulness of the tests for their purposes." In such studies, analysis of scores made by the same students as they progress through the grades should be of interest. Validity statistics are also offered to show the relationships between *SCAT* and rank in graduating class. For the verbal section the coefficient was .52.

As to the items in the test, the analogies appear uniformly fair and apt. Inevitably, of course, a verbal analogy test is to an extent also a vocabulary test; thus a fourth grader unfamiliar with words like *luggage* or *comprehend* will not be able to recognize analogies in which those words are used. But, of course, every test in which the student must read something is in part a vocabulary test.

**Differential Aptitude Tests (DAT); Spelling, Language Usage and Verbal Reasoning**. Forms S and T. George K. Bennett, Harold G. Seashore and Alexander G. Wesman. New York: The Psychological Corporation, 1973.

These are three parts of a much larger battery designed to indicate, in a general way, vocational aptitude of students in grades 8-12. The Spelling test consists of 100 words which are to be designated as correctly or incorrectly spelled. It requires ten minutes. The Language Usage test, which requires twenty-five minutes, consists of sixty items in this form:

| Ain't we / | going to / | the office / | next week? |
|:---:|:---:|:---:|:---:|
| A | B | C | D |

The test-taker is to mark *A* on the answer sheet for this item because of the "error" in that segment.

*Estimate of Validity and Usefulness*

As is too often true of spelling tests, this one requires only the recognition of rightness or wrongness, which is hardly the same as spelling the word. After all, recognizing a cauliflower is hardly the same as growing a cauliflower.

In an earlier edition of the usage test, many of the items were extremely trivial. This edition is a decided improvement, with nearly all of the "wrong" items being of the sort that would be rather offensive in formal communication.

Students are told, "If you do well on this test [Spelling] and on Language Usage, as well as on Verbal Reasoning, you should be able to do almost any kind of practical writing, provided you have a knowledge of your topic and a desire to write about it." True, no doubt. But the claim that the usage test "is among the best general predictors of course grades in high school and college" makes one wonder whether high schools and colleges tend too much to reward mastery of superficial form rather than substance.

*Verbal Reasoning Test*

This test consists of fifty items of the form "_____is to water as eat is to _____" followed by five pairs of words. The working time for this test is thirty minutes.

*Estimate of Validity and Usefulness*

The *DAT* battery is intended chiefly for use in counseling of students. Recommendations can be made concerning general kinds of occupations for which the battery suggests they are suited. The Verbal Reasoning test alone would not be very helpful to either a counselor or an English teacher, although the probability would seem to be that a student scoring high in it would be successful in college or in any kind of work requiring verbal competence and reasoning. Students are told that anyone with a combined rating at the 75th percentile or better in the verbal reasoning and numerical tests "should consider himself capable of peforming well in college courses"; a rating above the 50th percentile "also indicates college potential"; but it is "arguable" whether students in the third quarter should undertake liberal arts and science programs.

**Essentials of English Tests.** Forms A and B. Dora V. Smith and Constance M. McCullough (revised 1961 by Carolyne Greene). Circle Pines, Minn.: American Guidance Service, 1940 and 1961.

The test has five parts, with possible raw scores as follows: Spelling, 25; Grammatical Usage, 44; Word Usage, 15; Sentence Structure, 20; and Punctuation and Capitalization, 53. The Spelling test requires the test-taker to decide whether a word is or is not spelled correctly and to rewrite it if incorrect. The Grammatical Usage test presents questioned items in paragraph context; most of the items are verbs and pronouns. The test-taker writes the "correct" form of each item he or she considers wrong. In Word Usage, the student hunts out and corrects expressions like *off of* and *party* (for *person*). The Sentence Structure test asks the student to select from a group of four sentences the one that "most correctly and effectively states the idea." The Punctuation-Capitalization test requires the student to insert punctuation marks or capital letters where needed in two passages, one of which is a letter. The total working time for the test is forty-five minutes.

## Estimate of Validity and Usefulness

This is an unpretentious test. The *Manual of Directions* consists of six pages, which cover succinctly what some testmakers include in two or three booklets of twenty or thirty pages each. "The authors," says the manual, "are more concerned that teachers interest themselves in the performance of individual pupils than in any group comparisons." Hence, a Diagnostic Key to Error is provided to guide the teacher in deciding what points to stress with the whole class, and in suggesting "the manner in which individual pupils should be grouped in order to accommodate individual needs." This emphasis is laudable. If, for instance, no children in a class have difficulty with such verbs as *come* and *see*, why should class time be wasted on instruction in the usage of those verbs?

One may quibble with some of the test items. For instance, an eating place is named "the dog in the bun"; the student is to write this as "the Dog-in-the-Bun," and loses a point if he or she leaves out the hyphens. Are the hyphens really needed, and if they are, is a commercial establishment likely to use them? (I recall no hyphens in Chock Full o' Nuts.) The *what* in "I didn't know but what he would refuse" should be changed to *that* according to the test, but Bergen and Cornelia Evans, in *A Dictionary of Contemporary American Usage,* say that "*who knows but what it's all true,* is acceptable English in the United States." Multiple answers are also defensible for a few of the items in the Sentence Structure segment. And the allocation of over a third of the items to punctuation and capitalization seems unreasonably high.

In general, despite a few such quibbles, these simple, uncluttered tests are at least as good as others whose publishers have developed much more paraphernalia.

**Fundamental Achievement Series (FAS), Verbal**. Form B. George K. Bennett and Jerome E. Doppelt. New York: The Psychological Corporation, 1969.

The *FAS* tests are advertised as "culture-relevant," "fair to the disadvantaged," "based on everyday experiences that simulate real life situations and demands. Can the worker tell which bus will take him to work? . . . Does he understand commonly used words?" The tests are administered orally by means of tape-recordings "to enable those with limited reading skills to demonstrate their true abilities." Many "easy" questions were "deliberately included." Form A is sold only to personnel departments for testing of applicants and employees, but form B is also available to educators. Besides the Verbal tests, a Numerical test is included in the battery.

The Verbal test includes reading of rather ordinary signs and directions (e.g., "Shake well before using"), reading a menu, finding information in an apartment house list or a telephone book list, copying some very short sentences, answering questions about some short oral announcements, recognizing twenty-five correct or incorrect spellings of about the difficulty of *machine*, answering some simple questions concerning sets of four pictures, and finding in a multiple-choice test the best synonym for each of twenty-four words of about the difficulty of *economical*. The whole Verbal test takes about thirty minutes and consists of 100 items.

*Estimate of Validity and Usefulness*

This test is probably of greater use to an employer than to a school, which would have other means of discovering, for instance, whether a student can read a sign or copy a sentence. In general, the test seems well conceived, although the spelling section is subject to criticism. It represents a fourth of the whole test—a disproportionately large share—and, like so many other spelling tests, involves only recognizing rather than spelling.

**High School Placement Test**. Series 71E. Chicago: Science Research Associates, 1968.

The tests in this battery are Educational Ability (which includes vocabulary and verbal analogy items, plus arithmetic), Reading-

Language Arts Achievement, Arithmetic and Modern Mathematics Achievement, Social Studies Achievement, and Science Methodology. Purposes of the battery, which is intended for second-semester eighth graders and first-semester ninth graders, are to assist in placing students in appropriate curriculums, aid in ability grouping, and identify gifted or remedial students.

The Reading-Language Arts Achievement test consists of eighty-five items taking fifty minutes, divided about evenly between reading and language arts. The latter items "are designed to test skills in the use of the English language. The student must choose the alternatives that represent correct capitalization, punctuation, and spelling, the best grammatical usage, and effective expression. The student's actual use of the language, rather than his ability to memorize rules or definitions, is measured."

The test offers four selections of a few hundred words each. Certain words are underlined and the student is to indicate whether each underlined word or group of words is correct or in need of one of three suggested revisions. Then come questions testing how well the student read the passage; some of the reading questions are multiple-choice vocabulary items concerning words in the passage.

*Estimate of Validity and Usefulness*

Tests of usage, punctuation, and so on are of three basic types: those that ask the student to recognize whether an item is "right" or "wrong"; those that ask the student, after making such a decision, to choose the best correction for each "wrong" item; and those that require the student to *do* rather than just to recognize. Because of problems of scoring, there are very few tests of the third kind. This *SRA* test is one of the second kind, but it does not truly measure "the student's actual use of the language," despite the claim quoted above.

The reading selections on which the test items are based are moderately difficult for junior high ages; a fairly high percentage of students will be almost completely baffled by them. The language items themselves are a mixture of the reasonably significant and the trivial; occasionally, an item was obviously concocted by a teacher or an editor who didn't realize that no child is likely to write such a thing, e.g., "Some *merely* of these sculptors design their works. . . ." Also, some of the synonyms to be chosen as "correct" are rather off the mark. Despite such flaws, the publisher reports high correlations, averaging about .60 between test scores and course grades in two schools.

**Hoyum-Sanders Junior High School English Test.** Test I, forms A and B; and Test II, forms A and B. Vera D. Hoyum and M. W. Sanders. Emporia, Kans.: Bureau of Educational Measurements, 1964.

Each form consists of 135 items and requires forty minutes for answering. The divisions are as follows: Part I, sentence structure (what part of a sentence, if any, contains an error?), ten items; Part II, capitalization, fifteen items; Part III, punctuation, twenty-five items; Part IV, contractions, possessives, and spelling, fifteen items; Part V, grammar and usage (recognizing errors, choosing the correct word, and choosing the explanation of why it is correct), sixty items; and Part VI, alphabetization, ten items.

*Estimate of Validity and Usefulness*

All tests, probably, have to be contrived, but this one seems more so than most. What junior high student would debate whether to say "had flown" or "had flied"? Many might say "had flew," but that option isn't given. What junior high student would write "had slided" or "The balloon rised"? How realistic for junior high school is the choice "[1. Whoever 2. Whomever] Charles challenges, he defeats"? And what junior high student in "real life," as distinct from life conceived by testmakers, would ever have to wonder about which part of this group of words, if any, contains an error? "(1) How quickly change (2) from one (3) form (4) to another!"

This test hardly represents the apex of the art.

**Iowa Placement Examinations, English Training.** Series ET-2, form M. M. F. Carpenter, G. D. Stoddard, and L. W. Miller (revised by M. F. Carpenter and D. B. Stuit). Iowa City: Bureau of Educational Research and Service, 1941 and 1944.

This forty-five-minute test consists of three parts. Part 1, Spelling, consists of seventy-five words in four versions for each; the student selects the correct spelling. Part 2, Punctuation, has seventy-five rightly or wrongly punctuated sentences. Part 3, English Usage, offers seventy-five sentences that may or may not contain errors in usage.

*Estimate of Validity and Usefulness*

This old test is no better and no worse than many newer ones. The wrong spellings seem more lifelike than some of those conjured up for other tests. The principles of punctuation that are represented are unnecessarily repetitious. The English usage section has its share of almost impossible sentences like "I am not one who they could not interest in the fate of this gallant little band of heroes" and "Why have you lain idle all day?" Sometimes it's better to lie idle than to take a test like this.

**Iowa Tests of Basic Skills**. Levels 13 and 14, form 6. A. N. Hieronymus and E. F. Lindquist. Boston: Houghton Mifflin Co., 1971.

The complete battery consists of eight levels (numbered 7-14) for grades 1.7-2.5 through 8-9, covering vocabulary, reading comprehension, language skills, work-study skills, and mathematics skills. Only the vocabulary and language skills tests for Levels 13 and 14 (grades 7 and 8-9) were examined.

Items overlap for the various grade levels. For instance, some of the Level 11 and 12 items carry over into 13, and some of the Level 12 and 13 items carry over into 14. In the vocabulary test, the forty-eight items require seventeen minutes. Each item is multiple choice, in the following form:

*Close* the door
(1) shut  (2) hold  (3) behind  (4) open

The language skills tests are as follows:

Spelling: forty-eight items, twelve minutes, in the form "(1) our (2) mi (3) your (4) them (5) No mistakes."

Capitalization: forty-three items, fifteen minutes, in the form "(1) Tom and jerry (2) picked up all the (3) trash from the picnic. (4) No mistakes."

Punctuation: forty-three items, twenty minutes, in the form "(1) We all fasten (2) our seat belts (3) before, we leave. (4) No mistakes."

Usage: thirty-two items, twenty minutes, in the form "(1) He showed us the way. (2) Are you afraid to try? (3) Me and him took turns. (4) No mistakes."

## Estimate of Validity and Usefulness

As the title *Iowa Tests of Basic Skills* indicates, these are just tests of skills—only incidentally or coincidentally tests of knowledge, reasoning ability, or intelligence. An ideal test of skills would require the student to perform acts showing mastery of each skill; these may be unavoidably substitute recognition of other people's mastery or lack of it. For example, the student is not required to punctuate but only to determine whether someone else's sentences are correctly punctuated.

The employment of overlapping levels seems wise. A seventh grader, for instance, encounters test items both a little easier and a little harder than most seventh graders can cope with, so that his or her individual level of skills can be pretty accurately determined.

Almost without exception the individual test items appear suitable for the junior high grades. In vocabulary, for instance, such students should be able to define words like *corridor* or *tolerate*. In spelling, the misspellings represented are of the sort that students often make: *decieve* and *knowlege*, for example. In capitalization and punctuation, items may include unnecessary capitals or marks as well as incorrectly used ones. The usage items emphasize pronouns and verbs (which cause students most problems), but pay some attention to adjectives and adverbs, double negatives, redundancies, confusion of homonyms, and miscellaneous word forms such as *sheeps* for *sheep*.

Fewer than usual items are subject to criticism. In punctuation, though, there is an occasional item in which corrections in two lines, instead of the specified one, could be justified. In capitalization, several items are of the *Caspian sea* type, in which the test-takers are to indicate that *sea* is wrong; however, respectable journalistic practice would retain the small letter.

The *Teacher's Guide* suggests three possible plans for administering the tests: graded testing (e.g., all seventh graders take Level 13); out-of-level testing (giving a lower-level test to a slow group, a higher-level test to an academically superior group); individualized testing (giving each student the level of test that seems most appropriate for him or her). Although graded testing affords comparability of scores, the other choices allow for considerable flexibility.

The *Teacher's Guide* also offers suggestions for helping classes or individual students to improve in their areas of weakness. At least one of the suggestions concerning usage instruction is highly questionable: "Call the attention (orally, since sound is important in usage) of the pupils to their errors. Contrast the correct form with the one to be avoided." Following this suggestion might lead to frequent interruption of students, to interference with the flow of their thoughts, to emphasis upon "correctness" rather than content, and to reinforcement of the stereotype that English teachers' chief interest is in catching people making mistakes.

**Iowa Tests of Educational Development (ITED), SRA Assessment Survey**. Forms X-5 and Y-5. E. F. Lindquist and Leonard S. Feldt. Chicago: Science Research Associates, 1970.

The full *ITED* battery consists of tests in reading, language arts, mathematics, social studies, science, and use of sources. The tests are "designed to measure achievement in basic curriculum areas taught in grades 9-12 today. Tests require students to think critically, analyze written and illustrative materials, recognize statements of fundamental concepts, and select appropriate examples and applications of concepts. Recall of isolated information is given little emphasis."

The language arts test consists of fifty-four items on usage (broadly defined) and forty on spelling. The directions for the usage test serve to describe it:

The passages that follow might have been written by high school students. In the first two passages certain parts are underlined and numbered. In the right-hand column there are several choices with the same number as the underlined part. You are to choose the version that best expresses the idea, makes the statement grammatically correct or most precise, or is worded most consistently with the style and tone of the passage. Some items involve more than one kind of error. For example, you may find both grammatical and capitalization errors in the same item. In some cases the problem is not to correct a specific error, but to decide which phrase is most appropriate, considering the situation as a whole.

The final twelve items deal mainly with paragraph structure.

The spelling test consists of groups of four words, one of which may be spelled incorrectly. The student is asked to select the misspelling or to indicate that none is wrong.

The total language arts test requires forty minutes testing time. The same test is intended for all grades, 9 through 12; that is, there is not a separate test for each grade. The existence of two forms makes possible a comparison of scores at whatever time interval is desired. Only form X-5 was examined for this review.

### Estimate of Validity and Usefulness

The kinds of items covered in the usage test are summarized as follows in the *Handbook for Teachers and Examiners:*

|                                    | Form X-5 | Form Y-5 |
| ---------------------------------- | -------- | -------- |
| Capitalization and punctuation     | 10       | 10       |
| Verbs, adverbs, nouns              | 9        | 11       |
| Sentence structure                 | 9        | 9        |
| Appropriateness of writing         | 7        | 8        |
| Conciseness and clarity            | 12       | 11       |
| Organization and development       | 7        | 5        |

These figures suggest that if an examiner wants a test with major emphasis on capitalization, punctuation, and use of conventional verbs and pronouns, he or she should look elsewhere, since other tests under review have substantially more items on these topics. But if the examiner wants a broader, though shallower, view that includes the last four features in the list above, he or she should consider this test seriously. Since those four factors are significant, especially for their applicability to writing, the makers of this survey test were wise to include them.

"In many situations [in this test] the primary issue is one of style and fluency rather than clear-cut error," says the *Handbook*. Good. In actual student writing such flaws usually outnumber the definite "errors" that textbooks tend to concentrate on, but few tests tend to pay much attention to matters of style and fluency.

"An attempt has been made to avoid usage and practice on which there is substantial disagreement between language authorities." Good again. Other reviews in this book show that not all testmakers follow this principle consistently.

"The test . . . does not cover many elementary skills previously mastered by almost all high school students." If, then, some of your students say "they was," this test won't show you that. "The test must be considered primarily a survey test, and clues or indicators of particular student weaknesses must be corroborated by careful follow-up investigation."

"The present test is to be considered a complement to, not a substitute for, evaluations of student compositions." Some testmakers seem to imply that a usage test can tell a teacher how well each of his or her students writes. Not so, of course, since writing consists of much more than usage choices. As Lindquist and Feldt recognize, even a relatively broad test like this can reflect only a few of the characteristics of a student's ability to use the language.

The spelling test is not unusual in format. The words included are among those that most often are found in lists of common misspellings.

Like most other tests, the *ITED* stress the ability to recognize rather than the ability to do. But these tests have fewer flaws than the majority.

**Kansas Junior High School Spelling Test**. Test I, forms A and B, and Test II, forms A and B. Mary T. Williams, M. W. Sanders, Connie Moritz, and Alice Robinson. Emporia, Kans.: Bureau of Educational Measurements, 1964.

Each form covers eighty-five words and requires fifteen minutes to complete. Four spellings of each of the words are given; the student selects the correct one. Words included were selected with the aid of the *Buckingham Extension of the Ayres Spelling Scale*, the *Iowa Spelling Scale*, the Thorndike word list, and "a number of recognized spelling texts."

*Estimate of Validity and Usefulness*

The words appear about right for junior high level, but some of the misspellings appear farfetched; misspellings actually written by a number of students should be used rather than apparently dreamed-up misspellings like *rcail (racial), triangl, phresh,* and *rhbarbb (rhubarb)*. Probably, though, misspellings should not be used at all in a spelling test, because of their possibly being remembered; after looking at 1,360 misspellings in the four forms of this test, this reviewer had difficulty in spelling the word *errors*. (Is it *errorz*, or *erors*, or *airrirs*, all listed among the possibilities?) It is difficult to argue (*argu, aregu, rgue*) that test designers cannot find some better measure (*maysure, meashure, masure*)—one that would require actual spelling of words rather than just (1) *reconition* (2) *recogntion* (3) *recognishun* (4) *recognition*.

**Illinois Tests in the Teaching of English, Knowledge of Language**. Competency test A.   William H. Evans and Paul H. Jacobs. Carbondale, Ill.: Southern Illinois University Press, 1972. (See Purves review p. 130 for Knowledge of Literature test.)

This test differs from the others under review in that it is intended only for teachers or for college students preparing to become teachers. Other tests in the battery are Attitude and Knowledge in Written Composition, Knowledge of Literature, and Knowledge of the Teaching of English. The tests were developed noncommercially, under a federal grant, as one segment of a statewide effort in Illinois to upgrade preparation of teachers of English. Experimental editions of the tests were field tested in various colleges and universities, and "fifty nationally known experts," listed in the *Test Administrator's Manual*, offered critical analyses.

The language test consists of eighty-four multiple-choice items. The items pertain to "statements and terms used to describe how language functions, . . . the principles of semantics, . . . three systems of English grammar, . . . history of the English language, including its phonological, morphological, and syntactic changes, and concepts about levels of usage and dialectology, including the cultural implications of both." The test is not timed, although the time usually required is forty-five to sixty minutes.

*Estimate of Validity and Usefulness*

Some of the items involve rather philosophical points, such as a satisfactory definition of language or criteria for the value or worth of a language. Others probe the teacher's awareness of the most important tasks of the semanticist, the lexicographer, or some other variety of language scholar. Historical questions concern matters like lexicography and spelling, not just phonology, morphology, and syntax. The questions about dialects tend not toward specific points, such as variant pronunciations or lexical items, but toward an assessment of the teacher's attitudes toward dialect and his or her understanding of principles of dialectology. In its grammatical questions the test assumes that the test-taker is acquainted with all three of the present major descriptions of the language; it asks about characteristics of each and offers items that require the test-taker to apply certain principles of each of the grammars.

In other words, this test is totally unlike a test for students, which conventionally gets only into matters of "right" vs. "wrong" or—especially in the past—into grammatical identification of subjects, predicates, etc. This test for teachers probes much deeper and measures the teacher's familiarity with underlying philosophies of language and competing descriptions of it. This is as it should be, for the teacher who knows only such things as the rules for *was* and *were* and the superficial distinctions between a phrase and a clause will inevitably be shallow in the teaching of the language.

The test is not an easy one, nor should it be, since language has so many ramifications and complexities. In a preliminary seventy-eight-item version, no prospective teacher of English among 245 answered more than 62 correctly; the low score was 25. Inevitably, in a test that is simultaneously as broad in coverage and as deep as this, scores will not be high. But a teacher who can score 60 or so will assuredly be one whose teaching of the language can be far superior to that of the teacher whose knowledge is quite superficial—other things being equal.

The *Handbook* recommends five possible uses for the tests in this battery: (1) in preservice education, as an aid to academic and professional advising; (2) during early training in the field (student teaching or the first year of internship or full-time teaching); (3) for self-assessment (which teachers typically do too little of); (4) for assessment of applicants for teaching positions; and (5) during or after inservice workshops.

If all teachers of English during at least one of these stages were to be measured by this test and others in the battery, it seems likely that within a few years the level of preparation would begin to rise dramatically.

**Content Evaluation Series Language Arts Tests, Language Ability Test**. Form 1. Ellen Graser (Kellogg W. Hunt, series editorial adviser). Boston: Houghton Mifflin Co., 1969. (See Braddock review p. 122 for Composition test and Purves review p. 133 for Literature test.)

Intended for grades 7-9, the *"Language Ability Test* seeks to assess (1) the student's grasp of important principles underlying the construction of the English sentence and (2) the student's ability to use sentence elements in standard sentence patterns. To realize those objectives, the test concentrates on the distinctive areas which research has shown to be of greatest importance in language development—namely, sentence structure, word form and function, mechanics, and diction." Working time for the fifty-eight items is forty minutes. The test "does not try to measure how well a student can define and classify the elements of language, nor try to measure how well he can use technical terms to describe the functions of such elements." Nor does it insist that the only choices that can ever be made in a language test are "right" and "wrong."

As a result of these intentions, the author has put together a test that is unusual and unusually hard to describe. The items are of perhaps a dozen different kinds, of which fewer than half are concerned with the conventions of punctuation, capitalization, spelling, and usage. The others attempt to probe students' understanding of how sentences function, through asking them to think about which words might be substituted for which; which sentences in ordinary language follow the same patterns as sentences with nonsense words; what reply (in standard English) would be suitable to a question like "When will the roff be kunkeled?" or a command like "Never raddel the crompums"; and which standard English sentence is put together in the same way as another standard English sentence on an entirely different subject.

*Estimate of Validity and Usefulness*

The teacher who wants to know only how well his or her students can spell or punctuate or identify complex sentences will not like this test, for it won't do that. But the teacher who is especially interested in how well his or her students really have a *working understanding* of sentence construction will find it enlightening. And both teachers, by studying this test and the manual's discussion of its contents, may learn things that will benefit their teaching.

**McGraw-Hill Basic Skills System Spelling and Vocabulary Tests**. Form A. Alton L. Raygor. Monterey, Calif.: McGraw-Hill Book Co., 1970. (See Braddock review p. 123 for Writing test.)

In each of the fifty items in this twenty-minute test for grades 10-13, the student encounters four different underlined words in sentence context. One of the four words may be misspelled; the other three, though spelled correctly, are taken from lists of frequently misspelled words.

## Estimate of Validity and Usefulness

Anyone who prepares a published test and manual should be meticulous. In explaining that the words in this test were chosen on the basis of an extensive study, the author of the manual states, "Dr. Thomas Pollack reported this study in the *Journal of College English. . . .*" It shouldn't be *Pollack*; it's *Pollock*—a distinguished professor, university administrator, and past president of NCTE whose name anyone writing about spelling should be able to spell correctly (the name is misspelled at least five times in the manual, and correctly once). And it shouldn't be *Journal of College English*; it's *College English*. When the author refers so carelessly or sloppily to his basic source, one wonders how much trust can be placed in his test.

Actually, it has some good qualities, even though, as usual, it's a spelling test that doesn't require the student to spell. Giving the words in context makes possible the differentiation of words like *personal-personnel*. Also, it's probably better to have only one misspelling to three correct spellings rather than the other way around. The distractor words, too, as noted above, are themselves words often misspelled.

The test has two six-minute sections. Section 1 consists of thirty words chosen from beginning college textbooks in various fields; four possible synonyms are given for each. Section 2 has twenty-five "artificial words, created from parts whose meanings are well established." For example:

> pyrophile:   1. a blacksmith's tool   2. a builder of pyramids
> 3. one who loves fire   4. one who tells lies

## Estimate of Validity and Usefulness

Section 1 is ordinary in concept and execution; the words seem appropriate for grades 10-13 and are drawn from both the sciences and the humanities and arts. Section 2, however, offers a praiseworthy and interesting departure from the ordinary. The student who has a good vocabulary and who has thought much about words will associate "pyrophile," for instance, with words like *pyromania* and *bibliophile*, and come up with the desired answer, "one who loves fire." Thus this part of the test should be an excellent indicator of vocabulary strength.

**Minnesota High School Achievement Examinations, Language Arts.** Tests 1-6, form EH. V. L. Lohmann, editor. Circle Pines, Minn.: American Guidance Service, 1974.

The total battery consists of twenty-six achievement tests for junior and senior high schools. There are separate Language Arts tests for each grade, 7 through 12. The manual claims that "the questions selected for the test reflect the ever-changing Minnesota courses of study. . . ." Thus the tests are geared specifically to Minnesota users, but are also "generally applicable," according to the manual, to other states.

Classes of items vary somewhat from grade to grade. Thus grade 8 has items on spelling (fifteen); vocabulary (twenty); kinds of sentences (i.e., declarative, etc., nineteen); capitalization and punctuation (twelve); grammatical usage (finding errors in, ten); usage of words (ten); faulty expression (five); verb tense (ten); kinds of sentences (i.e., simple, etc., nine); grammatical terms (e.g., completing a definition of a grammatical term, fifteen); and literature (twenty-five). Grade 12 repeats several of these, though in somewhat varied fashion, but also has entries on library skills (mostly indicating sources of information, fifteen) and composition (e.g., finding the "best" sentence, twenty-eight).

*Estimate of Validity and Usefulness*

These tests are poor in conception and in execution. Certainly language arts—especially in Minnesota, where Dora V. Smith and Harold Allen have labored so diligently—devotes less attention than these tests suggest to sentence classification, tense identification, and sorting out parts of speech. Certainly Minnesota teachers would not uniformly agree that "a real good time" is definitely an error in usage. And how important is it for an eighth-grader to know Ichabod Crane's occupation? These tests are revised rather frequently. It is hoped that future editions will be better.

**Missouri College English Test**. Form A. Robert Callis and Willoughby Johnson. New York: Harcourt, Brace & World, 1964.

Only form A was examined for this report. It is "for general college use and for use with high school seniors." Form B "is reserved for use in colleges and universities exclusively." Form C is for "situations demanding a 'secure' test."

The test consists of ninety items and requires forty minutes. Two-thirds of the items involve spotting errors in paragraph context, in punctuation, capitalization, "grammar," and spelling. Ten items require students to find the best sentence in a group of four. The remaining twenty items are sentences in four scrambled paragraphs that the student is to place in the best possible order.

*Estimate of Validity and Usefulness*

Despite its emphasis on location of errors, this is one of the best available tests for high school upperclassmen or college freshmen. The passages in which the "errors" are embedded appear more realistic, less concocted than most; some are indeed doctored versions of student writing. The "find-the-best-sentence" items are interesting and challenging; again the poor sentences seem realistic. Ability to rearrange the scrambled paragraphs is a fine measure of a student's understanding of principles of organization.

During development of the test, whenever it was found "that the large majority of beginning college freshmen had already mastered the knowledge or skill being measured by a particular item, that item was omitted even though it was logically a part of the domain. . . . Thus the test comprises those items considered by competent judges to be valid measures of specified skills and abilities not yet fully mastered by the majority of beginning college freshmen." The list of punctuation and "grammar" items that survived this screening is informative: punctuation between independent clauses, with parenthetical, restrictive, and nonrestrictive elements, and to show possession; verbs (agreement, tense, principal parts); pronouns (case, relative, reference); adverbs distinguished from adjectives; and special cases.

A truly superior test, of course, would measure the student's ability to do rather than to recognize. It also might include some kinds of items (e.g., vocabulary) that this test does not. But until the superior test comes along, this one is a pretty good substitute.

**Sanders-Fletcher Spelling Test**. Test I, forms A and B; and Test II, forms A and B. Gwen Fletcher and M. W. Sanders. Emporia, Kans.: Bureau of Educational Measurements, 1964.

Each form, to be used in grades 9-13, covers 150 words. The first ninety are in a list, with about half of them misspelled; the student is to decide which ones. Part II presents twenty-five pairs of words, like *stationary* and *stationery*, in sentences; the student chooses the one required by the sentence. In Part III, the student faces groups of five different words (e.g., *"clique, detergent, predjudice, trek, debtor"*), with the one misspelled to be selected.

*Estimate of Validity and Usefulness*

Some of the misspellings appear unlikely, e.g., *prohesied*. However, more serious is the fact that some spellings considered wrong are recognized as alternative spellings in *Webster's Third: propellor, liquify,* and *payed* (at least in the sense of "payed out the rope"). The trouble with most spelling tests, including this one, is that they measure something other than spelling ability. They measure the ability to *recognize* a spelling as correct or incorrect; this is by no means the same thing as the ability to write a word correctly.

Another weakness of many spelling tests, including this one, is that they do not diagnose at all the kinds of spelling troubles that a given student has. The test authors admit as much in the manual, where they say, not very helpfully, "Should it be found that some students have difficulties which cannot be readily located by use of this test, several diagnostic tests should be obtained or constructed and administered. After the specific weaknesses and handicaps are located, remedial measures may be applied intelligently." So what's the use of giving this test?

**Sanders-Fletcher Vocabulary Test**. Test I, forms A and B; and Test II, forms A and B. Gwen Fletcher and M. W. Sanders. Emporia, Kans.: Bureau of Educational Measurements, 1964.

Constructed for grades 9-13, each of the four forms requires forty minutes for answering and consists of 100 items. Seventy-five of the items are multiple choice, asking students to choose the best definition among five possibilities; twenty-five items require only a plus or a minus to indicate proper or improper use of a word. Words in the test were chosen from the Pressey lists of basic vocabulary in a number of high school subjects and from "other supplementary lists." Words were checked against the Thorndike word lists in an attempt to make the various forms comparable in difficulty.

### Estimate of Validity and Usefulness

It is difficult to defend a few of the word choices. How important is it, for instance, that a student know *dudgeon, gimp, counterpane, marzipan, snickersnee, veldt,* and *Caledonia?* Some such words certainly deserve inclusion to determine the vocabulary level of the occasional widely-read student. Most of the words are of the approximate levels of *dexterous* and *mundane.*

The authors say that test results may be used "(1) for determining pupil achievement; (2) for checking the efficiency of instruction; (3) for analyzing pupil and class weakness; and (4) for motivating pupil effort." They add that if a student's paper is studied, his or her weaknesses may be found and "remedial measures may be applied intelligently." It is difficult to agree with these statements unless the class has been engaged specifically in vocabulary study that happens to have included the words in these tests. And if a student's test shows that he or she doesn't know *marzipan* and *counterpane* and the like, just what "remedial measures may be applied intelligently" except to encourage him or her—like every other student—to read more books, see more places, do more kinds of work, play a greater variety of games, have more experiences?

Essentially the same claims of usefulness, incidentally, are used for other tests in this series, generally in identical words. Yet a vocabulary test *should* have somewhat different uses than, say, a test of sentence structure, usage, or punctuation.

**Cooperative Sequential Tests of Educational Progress (STEP), Listening.** Forms 1A, 1B, 2A, 2B, 3A, 3B, 4A, and 4B. Princeton, N.J.: Educational Testing Service, 1957. (See Braddock review p. 125 for Writing test.)

Other tests in this battery covering grades 4-14 include reading, writing, essay, social studies, science, and mathematics. Each Listening test consists of two thirty-five-minute segments, with thirty-six or forty items in each segment. The administrator reads a short passage aloud, typically about two minutes for each of twelve passages. The student's test booklet provides several multiple-choice questions on the passage.

The test, says the manual, "Measures ability, through listening to passages read by the teacher or test administrator, to comprehend main ideas and remember significant details, to understand the implications of the ideas and details, and to evaluate and apply the material presented. Materials include directions and simple explanation, exposition, narration, argument and persuasion, and aesthetic material (both poetry and prose)."

*Estimate of Validity and Usefulness*

The selections for student listening are likely to be of at least reasonable interest to most students, and they vary greatly in style and content. None requires much more than three minutes of listening time. (If a teacher wants to measure the ability to listen to and retain information about a considerably longer selection, the *Brown-Carlsen Listening Comprehension Test*, discussed earlier, should be considered.) The questions are intelligent and not excessively picky. They do measure, as the quotation from the manual states, much more than the recollection of detail. A recording of the passages to be listened to might be preferable to reading by the teacher, especially if test results are to be compared with norms or with results in classes of other teachers.

**Stanford Achievement Test (SAT).** Primary Level II, Intermediate Level I, Advanced, and Test of Academic Skills; form A. Richard Madden, Eric F. Gardner, Herbert C. Rudman, Bjorn Karlsen, and Jack C. Merwin. New York: Harcourt Brace Jovanovich, 1973. (See Purves review p. 128 for *SAT* High School Arts and Humanities test.)

In all, the *SAT* covers six levels. Not reviewed here are Primary Level I, mainly for grades 1.6-2.5; Primary Level III, mainly for grades

3.6-4.5; and Intermediate Level II, mainly for grades 5.6-6.9. There is also a Stanford Test of Academic Skills ("Stanford TASK") intended for grades 9-13 and not included in this review.

Coverage of test batteries varies, but in general a battery includes vocabulary, reading comprehension, word study skills, spelling, language, mathematics, social science, and science. All the tests for a single level are contained in a single booklet.

Here is a summary of the contents of the three tests under review:

Primary Level II
> Vocabulary—Thirty-seven three-choice items, twenty minutes. Pupil marks the word that best fits into a sentence read by the teacher.
>
> Word Study Skills—Sixty-five three-choice items, twenty-five minutes. A. Pupil selects the word that matches what the teacher pronounces. B. Pupil matches a sound in one word with that in another.
>
> Spelling—Forty-three three-choice items, twenty-five minutes. Pupil indicates each spelling as "right," "wrong," or "don't know."
>
> Listening Comprehension—Fifty multiple-choice items, thirty-five minutes. Pupil follows instructions read by the teacher.

Intermediate Level I
> Vocabulary—Fifty multiple-choice items, twenty-five minutes. Pupil marks the word that best fits a sentence.
>
> Word Study Skills—Fifty-five multiple-choice items, twenty-five minutes. A. Pupil matches sounds. B. Pupil observes which syllables, when put together, will form words.
>
> Spelling—Fifty multiple-choice items, fifteen minutes. A. Homonyms. B. Pupil chooses the one incorrect spelling in a group of four words.
>
> Language—Seventy-nine multiple-choice items, thirty-five minutes. A. Usage items include verbs, pronouns, punctuation, capitalization, and miscellaneous matters of diction. B. Pupil determines whether a group of words is a complete or an incomplete sentence. C. Pupil determines whether a group of words is a sentence, two sentences, or no sentence. D. Pupil answers questions on dictionary entries.

Advanced Level
> Vocabulary—Fifty multiple-choice items, twenty minutes. Pupil selects word that best finishes a sentence.

Spelling—Sixty multiple-choice items, twenty minutes. A. Homonyms. B. Pupil chooses the one incorrect spelling in a group of four words.

Language—Seventy-nine multiple-choice items, thirty-five minutes. A. Assorted usage items, in context. B. Pupil determines whether a group of words is a sentence, two sentences, or no sentence. C. Pupil answers questions on dictionary entries. D. Pupil answers several questions on reference books, literary concepts, and grammatical concepts.

## *Estimate of Validity and Usefulness*

Strong points of these tests include:

1. a practice test for the primary level to introduce small children to possibly unfamiliar kinds of tests;
2. vocabulary items that with few exceptions appear suitable for the indicated grade levels;
3. word study skills that are simple but basic and sometimes slightly imaginative in presentation;
4. spelling tests no worse than average;
5. an excellent listening comprehension test for the primary level, a test that may give some teachers ideas about why and how to teach this still-too-neglected skill;
6. language tests that stress such basic matters as verbs and pronouns and that measure to a reasonable extent pupils' ability to distinguish sentences from sentence fragments and run-ons. The testmakers have pretty well kept up with recent language study.

Weaknesses tend to be in a small number of individual items. A few usage items are subject to question, especially with regard to capitalization; for instance, the test insists on Center Street, even though journalistic style uses a small s. It insists also on the debatable King and Prime Minister of England. Also, in the sentence-identification segments of the Language test for both intermediate and advanced levels, fewer than a fifth of the items, instead of the expected third, are of the run-on variety so commonly found in school and even college writing. In the intermediate Language test, parts B and C overlap in purpose and method. One test insists on a comma after an introductory adverbial clause even when the clause is rather short and there is no chance of misreading; editors of reputable magazines often omit the comma in such a case. In another part of a language test, pupils are asked whether their fingernails rattle, chatter, whistle, or screech on the blackboard; this reviewer tried to find out empirically and succeeded in attaining a rattle, a screech, and even a sort of whistle, and hence finds that item confusing. Perhaps some of the vocabulary words in the Advanced test are a bit stiff for eleven- to fourteen-year-olds: *quiescence, conclave,* and *anomalous,* for instance, but maybe those words are needed to accommodate the few people who would otherwise leap off the top of the scale. And these testmakers, like others, have still not found a really satisfactory spelling test, although the words they use are better chosen than most and the misspellings are among those that children actually write.

Despite such little flaws, these tests should certainly be included among those to be considered by an elementary, middle, or junior high school interested in obtaining a reasonably comprehensive understanding of pupils' individual achievements in the academic areas considered here.

**Tests of Academic Progress, Composition.** Form S. Dale P. Scannell, Boston: Houghton Mifflin Co., 1971. (See Purves review p. 135 for Literature test.)

The Composition tests for the four grades are contained in the same booklet, with overlapping items. That is, grade 9 does exercises 1-64; grade 10, 19-83; grade 11, 47-111; and grade 12, 65-130. In general, the lower numbered exercises refer mainly to mechanics and verb and pronoun usage, and the later exercises pay more attention to paragraphing and slightly more difficult matters of mechanics and usage. The test consists of short prose pieces (e.g., a letter and a book report), followed by multiple-choice questions; lists of terms which are to be grouped together according to given categories; and nonsense verbs (e.g., "to neg") for which five tense forms are given, followed by sentences in which one of the forms must be inserted. About sixty-four items are done by each grade.

*Estimate of Validity and Usefulness*

The prose selections would be moderately interesting to high school students. The questions about paragraphing, however, are rather good. The device of making all grade level tests available in overlapping form could result in some interesting statistical comparisons within a school.

### Tests of Adult Basic Education. Forms M and D. Monterey, Calif.: California Test Bureau/McGraw-Hill Book Co., 1967.

These tests are adapted from the 1957 edition of *California Achievement Tests, WXYZ Series*, devised by Ernest W. Tiegs and Willis W. Clark. Other tests in the adult battery are in reading and arithmetic. Form M is of medium difficulty and form D, "difficult." (There is also a form E, "easy," but it has no language section.) In general, the tests are intended "to meet a growing need for instruments especially designed to measure adult achievement in the basic skills of reading, arithmetic, and language."

In form M, the first thirty-seven items refer to capitalization, with the test-taker expected to indicate each time which one of four words needs to be capitalized. In each of the next thirty-four items the test-taker indicates whether any mark of punctuation is needed. The next twenty-six items require a choice between pairs of words like *flew, flown* or *too, two* or *better, best.* Then come nine items that may or may not be sentence fragments. The test ends with thirty sets of four words, one of which may be misspelled. Total working time for the 136 items is thirty-eight minutes. Form D is similar in content.

*Estimate of Validity and Usefulness*

According to the manual, test items from the *California Achievement Tests* have been revised to make them more suitable for adults. The attempt is by no means completely successful, with its accounts of trips to New York with Mom and Dad, Tom's endeavor to wheedle a motorcycle out of Uncle Ed, and the like.

The amount of emphasis on capitalization and punctuation is excessive—71 of 136 items in form M, 59 of 129 in form D. The spelling test, like most others, involves recognition only. Some of the items in mechanics and usage are at best questionable. Must *river* be capitalized in *Missouri river*? Publishers' stylebooks differ on this, so why include the item? In *my aunt Betsy*, is it imperative that *aunt* be capitalized, as the scoring key says? After all, we don't write *my Brother Ben*. May *sunk* be used as past tense? *Webster's Third* says so, but not the makers of this test.

**Thurstone Test of Mental Alertness**. Forms A and B. Thelma G. and L. L. Thurstone. Chicago: Science Research Associates, 1952 (form A) and 1953 (form B).

As many as possible of the 126 items are to be finished in twenty minutes. Some ask for definitions in this way: "the letter that begins the name of the first meal of the day." Others are same-opposite, e.g., "What word means the same as or the opposite of the first word in the row: many A. ill B. few C. down D. sour."

*Estimate of Validity and Usefulness*

The test is intended to aid in the selection, placement, and evaluation of employees; in schools, it is said to reflect ability to comprehend complex material, forecast success in academic subjects, and afford a comparison with the scores of persons in vocational categories. Statistics in the manual suggest that the test performs these functions rather well. Male college graduates, for example, score considerably higher than automobile salesmen, most of whom, at least at the time of standardizing, were presumably not college graduates; but automobile salesmen score higher than retail sales personnel in general. Students' grade point averages correlate fairly closely with their test scores.

The vocabulary words in the test are of reasonable degrees of difficulty, e.g., *aqueous* but not *vitreous*. The number of items to be completed in twenty minutes requires fast reaction, i.e., alertness.

**Walton-Sanders English Test**. Test I, forms A and B; and Test II, forms A and B. Charles E. Walton and M. W. Sanders. Emporia, Kans.: Bureau of Educational Measurements, 1964.

There are three parts, totaling 150 items, in this fifty-minute test for grades 9-13. Part I, The Word, is subdivided into a twenty-five-item section on vocabulary (multiple-choice definitions); a fifteen-item section on syllabication (counting the number of syllables in a word); and a twenty-item section on spelling (finding the misspelled word in a group of five). Part II, The Sentence, has twenty items on identifying parts of speech; twenty items on use of nouns, pronouns, and adjectives within sentences; and fifteen items on identification of verbals. Part III consists of thirty-five items on punctuation.

*Estimate of Validity and Usefulness*

There is little value in counting syllables in a word, yet this represents a tenth of this test. The fifty-five items on the sentence all involve mere identification. There are no items on usage, and, as is true of many other tests, nothing on sentence construction. A test just like this could have been constructed at the turn of the century and would have reflected what at that time was happening in the classroom.

**Wide Range Achievement Test (WRAT), Revised Edition**. Levels I and II. J. F. Jastak, S. W. Bijou, and S. R. Jastak. Wilmington, Del.: Guidance Associates of Delaware, 1965.

The *WRAT* has sections on spelling, arithmetic, and reading. Level I is for ages 5 years through 11 years, 11 months; Level II, 12 through adult. In each test, easy items come first, with difficulty increasing steadily and rapidly.

The Level I spelling test consists of forty-five words from simple monosyllables to words that would be fairly difficult for junior high students. For younger students there are also brief sections involving the drawing of letter-shaped designs and the letters of the child's name. Level II has forty-six words and also starts with monosyllables, but moves in larger steps, ending with words that would not be in most high school students' vocabularies. Total scores for both tests are equated with typical grade levels; thus, a Level I adjusted score of 50 equals grade level 7.2. In giving the test, the examiner dictates the words in sentence context. Thus, this test, unlike most, actually requires the test-taker to write the word and not just recognize whether a spelling is correct or not.

*Estimate of Validity and Usefulness*

The manual devotes several pages to statistical evidence concerning the validity of the test. The evidence seems to show high correlations with other kinds of tests. A teacher who wants an estimate of how well a class or an individual spells in relation to national norms should find this test useful. It cannot, however, serve a diagnostic purpose; that is, the particular kinds of errors a given student or class makes cannot be accurately analyzed.

# Evaluation of Writing Tests

*Richard Braddock*

Unless one wishes to restrict one's conception of "writing" to the kind of essays employed in classrooms largely to test a student's understanding of a literary text or proficiency in avoiding certain "errors" covered by an English handbook, one sees writing as a staggeringly complicated and varied process. Some modes of writing are highly personal, like the kind found in self-initiated journals or individual pieces written to get something off the writer's chest or to record events or feelings for the writer's later reference. Unless the writer solicits the reactions of someone else to such writing, it is no one else's affair. Other writing, which seeks to communicate with readers removed in space or time, is a more public affair and at times may properly become the concern of the schools and even society at large. It is apparent that a writer's prospective readers may vary from an intimate friend who knows him or her well to a loosely defined category of people whom the writer has never seen and whose sense of values, set of experiences, and dialect of English differ from his or her own. Furthermore, a writer may have widely varying purposes from time to time: to explain to readers something about which the writer claims a special understanding; to get readers to share a feeling for something; to sell them something; to solicit their votes.

When "writing" is viewed as a varied and complicated concept, one readily sees that "writing ability" is a pair of words which has little meaning when taken in the abstract. Are there definable characteristics, understandings, and skills which are common to all modes of writing, for all kinds of prospective readers, for all possible purposes of writers? How can one consider "writing ability" in general when no one knows what it is? It may not even exist.

Of course there is a tendency for all types of writing to have common characteristics of sentence structure, word meaning, and mechanics (spelling, punctuation, capitalization, handwriting and typing, and general format). That this is no more than a tendency, though, is readily apparent to anyone who has compared these features in a scholarly article, an Uncle Remus story, and a cigaret ad. For some readers, the most communicative description of the plight of a black ghetto dweller may be cast in their own variety of English, not exclusively in the forms which English handbooks offer as standard. Still, one can say that standard English tends to have common characteristics if one is referring to the matters listed at the beginning of this paragraph. Accordingly, tests have been devised to indicate the degree to which students can distinguish between standard and nonstandard forms about which there is little disagreement. Even these tests must be revised from time to time, however, as people's consensus shifts about what is standard and what is not.

But to suggest that tests over such standard forms are tests of writing ability is patently absurd for two reasons. First, such tests sample students' ability to distinguish between standard and nonstandard forms which someone else has written, not their ability to write their own. At best, these tests evaluate proofreading ability or, more charitably but less accurately, editing ability. Second, such tests make no attempt to measure students' ability to accomplish other aspects of writing. No commercially available standardized test attempts to measure a student's ability to select a subject, and an approach and a mode for it appropriate to the writer and the prospective readers. No commercially available standardized test attempts to measure a student's ability to organize and detail his or her writing so that prospective readers can share the writer's experience and appreciate his or her purposes. At this stage of our understanding of writing and of testing, it is difficult to believe that any standardized test will be constructed which can measure such abilities. Therefore, anyone who professes to evaluate "writing ability" with a standardized test is either telling a falsehood or speaking from ignorance. It is a cruel joke that some corporations are today selling school boards on the notion that they can do just that. And it is ironic that some colleges are excusing students from composition requirements merely on the basis of standardized test scores.

Roughly predicting a student's ability to do well in a composition course is something else. If large numbers of students are to be tracked according to their proficiency in writing standard English, and if success in the tracks is judged heavily on that basis, then standardized test scores may have predictive value. Students who are misclassified by such tests can be reclassified after their teacher has had a chance to see several examples of their actual writing. But the use of standardized tests for tracking purposes at the beginning of a course should never lead anyone to use them to evaluate "writing ability" at the end of the course. That would be like using a ruler to measure the artistic quality of a painting.

What actually is included in commercially available tests that is purported to measure "writing ability"? Usually tests consist almost entirely of items concerned with sentence structure, word meaning, and mechanics. They never attempt to cope with a student's ability to select a subject, pursue a specific intention, and effectively address a particular audience. Occasionally, however, a test will include items which relate to a student's ability to judge the organization and substantive details of a piece of writing—even though, of course, the writing is not the student's and the prospective readers are usually not identified.

Three commercially available standardized tests which claim to measure "writing ability" were examined to see how many items concern aspects of writing which extend beyond the confines of a sentence, other than the reference of a pronoun to an antecedent in a preceding sentence. The three are *Tests of Academic Progress, Composition,* Form 1, Houghton Mifflin Company, 1964; *Basic Skills System Writing Test,* Form A, McGraw-Hill Book Company, 1970; and *Sequential Tests of Educational Progress, Writing,* Form 2B, Educational Testing Service, 1957 (referred to below as *STEP*).

The McGraw-Hill test was designed for grades 9-12, the *STEP* test for grades 10-12 (though forms for other levels are also available). The Houghton Mifflin test is organized in overlapping units to be taken by students at different levels: ninth graders take items 1-70, tenth graders 23-92, eleventh graders 47-117, and twelfth graders 71-142. No judgment is implied here of the suitability of a category of items or the effectiveness of particular items. For example, the McGraw-Hill test seems to imply that a topic sentence is always the first sentence in a paragraph, and it seems to leave no room for the possibility that some well-written paragraphs have no topic sentence. Moreover, good writers would disagree about which are the best answers for some items in all three tests and would not care to choose any of the possible answers as a "best" answer for a few of the items.

An interesting question arises as one examines the tests. What is the difference between a test of reading ability and a multiple-choice test of "writing ability"? If one did not wish to consider a student's ability to choose "standard" items in sentence structure and mechanics, could a student's success in a composition course be predicted just as well by using a good reading test instead of the tests considered here?

## References

Braddock, Richard, Lloyd-Jones, Richard, and Schoer, Lowell. *Research in Written Composition.* Urbana, Ill.: National Council of Teachers of English, 1963, pp. 40-45.

Diederich, Paul B. "How to Measure Growth in Writing Ability." *English Journal* 55 (April 1966): 435-449.

Godshalk, Fred I., Swineford, Frances, and Coffman, William E. *The Measurement of Writing Ability.* Research Monograph No. 6. Princeton, N.J.: College Entrance Examination Board, 1966. Also see the reviews of this publication and the response of its authors in "Roundtable Review," *Research in the Teaching of English* 1 (Spring 1967): 76-88.

Sherwood, John C., et al. "Terminal Report of the Committee on Testing." *College Composition and Communication* 17 (December 1966): 269-272.

**College English Placement Test (CEPT).** Oscar M. Haugh and James I. Brown. Boston: Houghton Mifflin Co., 1969.

The manual lists these four purposes for *CEPT*: (1) to measure reliably and quickly a student's ability to use the language effectively; (2) to provide accurate information for placing a student in the kind of composition class best suited to individual needs and abilities; (3) to indicate specific language areas needing further attention and study; and (4) to provide insights bearing on the entire process of written composition, from the selection of an appropriate subject to the final proofreading.

In order to achieve these purposes, the authors have constructed a 106-item, multiple-choice test and assignments for two short compositions that cannot be objectively scored. The objective test can be given independently of the writing and requires forty-five minutes. Coverage is unusually broad, including size of subject for a composition; arrangement of ideas; transitions; selection of most effective sentences; vocabulary (analogies, appropriateness to context); grammar of an irregular verb; and mechanics (capitalization, punctuation, spelling, forms of words).

*Estimate of Validity and Usefulness*

This test is much better than most. It should accomplish its designated purposes extraordinarily well. Items are clear, carefully worked out, and sometimes imaginative. Unlike many other tests, it is not grossly overbalanced in the most easily measured areas such as spelling and punctuation. It gets at important facets of writing— such as arrangement of ideas—and largely eschews trivia. Tests as good as this can be constructed for the lower schools, but few of them exist.

**Content Evaluation Series Language Arts Tests, Composition Test.** Form 1. Leonard Freyman (Kellogg W. Hunt, series editorial advisor). Boston: Houghton Mifflin Co., 1969. (See Hook review p. 103 for Language Ability test and Purves review p. 133 for Literature test.)

The aim of this test, covering grades 7-9, "is to assess the ability of the student to manipulate his language effectively—that is, to express himself correctly, clearly, and forcefully in a series of interrelated, meaningful sentences organized to bring out a central point. To realize this goal, the author has developed the test around the three principles of classical rhetoric—invention, organization, and style. Through a series of interesting, thought-provoking exercises, the author involves students in practical composition situations. To the degree that the student can meet the demands of those situations, he reveals his ability to express himself on a given topic."

The sixty items in this forty-minute test are considerably different from those in most composition tests. Here are questions on size of topic, arrangement of subtopics, organization of sentences in a paragraph, transitions, and relative effectiveness of various statements of the same idea. But there are not the usual ones about choosing between *her* and *she* or *did* and *done* or a semicolon and a comma.

*Estimate of Validity and Usefulness*

This is one of the best composition tests for the junior high school, because it emphasizes important matters rather than the usual inconsequentials. A student who does well on this test is ready for most writing assignments he or she is likely to get in high school; in fact, he or she may be more ready for college writing than many college freshmen are. This does not mean that the test is too difficult. It is not, for properly taught students. English courses that emphasize the kinds of writing instruction implied by this test will adequately prepare students not only for the test but—much more important—for later writing.

**McGraw-Hill Basic Skills System Writing Test.** Form A. Alton L. Raygor. Monterey, Calif.: McGraw-Hill Book Co., 1970. (See Hook review p. 104 for Spelling and Vocabulary tests.)

The three fifteen-minute segments of this test are devoted to Language Mechanics, Sentence Patterns, and Paragraph Patterns. For the first of these (thirty items), bits of a composition are underlined, and students are to indicate whether they find in each an error in capitalization, in punctuation, in "grammar," or no error. The sec-

ond part (twenty-six items) asks for identification of sentence fragments and simple, compound, and complex sentences; for the
"grammatically correct" sentence in a group of four; for the sentence in a group of four that shows parallel construction; and for the
most appropriate transition between sentences. The third part
(fifteen items) asks students to choose the best topic sentence for a
paragraph; the sentences best developing a given topic sentence; the
best concluding sentence; the best sequence of sentences in a paragraph; and the best places to start new paragraphs.

*Estimate of Validity and Usefulness*

The section devoted to paragraphs is ingenious and useful. It measures students' mastery of important concepts. The section on the
sentence is a peculiar amalgam. Aften ten not very useful identifications of sentence types (more than a third of the whole section), there
are five groups of four sentences, of which precisely one is said to be
correct in each group. This reviewer, however, finds two unimpeach-
able sentences in one group; in another, there is a grammatically
correct sentence, but the punctuation is unquestionably faulty. Several of the sentences in the parallel construction group are pretty
strained. The section on choice of transitions is well conceived but
imperfectly executed. In summary, measurement of students' mastery of sentence patterns apparently entails only identification of a
few sentence types plus recognition of satisfactory relative pronouns,
parallel structure, and transitions; in this test, some of the items
designed to measure those elements are poorly executed.

Worse, though, is the section on Language Mechanics. Here is an
exact parallel of one part:

> [1]Did you ever seen the story of [2]*Mr. Hyde* on television. [3]It stars
> Peter Lorre as the infamous [4]monster. Complete with gigantic
> teeth and [5]slobbovian accent.

Students are to indicate errors in capitalization, punctuation, and
grammar, or may mark "No error." Number 1 is a grammatical
error, but so farfetched as to be a worthless item. Number 2, the answer sheet says correctly, is an error in punctuation. Number 3, says
the answer sheet, is a grammatical error. Why, in heaven's name?
Number 4 is called an error in punctuation, as it is, but why penalize
the student who says it is an error in capitalization? Critical reading by a few experts in English could have quickly eliminated the
serious flaws in this test.

**Cooperative Sequential Tests of Educational Progress (STEP), Writing**. Forms 1A, 1B, 2A, 2B, 3A, 3B, 4A, and 4B. Princeton, N.J.: Educational Testing Service, 1957. (See Hook review p. 109 for Listening test.)

Other tests in the complete battery include reading, listening, essay (separate from the Writing test), social studies, science, and mathematics. The *STEP* tests are achievement tests that focus "on skill in solving new problems on the basis of information learned, rather than on ability to handle only 'lesson material.' "

The Writing test, says one of the several manuals accompanying *STEP*, "Measures ability to think critically in writing, to organize materials, to write material appropriate for a given purpose, to write effectively, and to observe conventional usage in punctuation and grammar. Materials were selected from actual student writing in letters, answers to test questions. . . ."

The test items for all grades are intended to go far beyond the usual emphasis on mechanics, or beyond even mechanics and organization. The proportion of items classified "on the basis of the *major* responses they demand" is as follows:

|  | Forms for Grades 4-6 (percent) | Forms for Grades 7-14 (percent) |
|---|---|---|
| Organization | 30 | 20 |
| Conventions | 20 | 20 |
| Critical thinking | 15 | 15 |
| Effectiveness | 20 | 30 |
| Appropriateness | 15 | 15 |

As these figures show, the test designers believed that in high school and college more attention should be given to effectiveness, less attention to organization. The *Teacher's Guide* classifies each item by placing it in one, and sometimes two, of these five categories.

Divided into two thirty-five minute segments, each Writing test consists of sixty multiple-choice items. "The passages on which groups of items are based are drawn largely from materials actually written by students in schools and colleges—assignments which by and large were graded poor or failing." Typically the questions are of this sort: "Which of the following would be the best version of Sentence X?" But there are many variations, such as "Which should come first?," "Which two parts of Paragraph 1 belong in the same sentence?,", and "Which of these sentences contains a misspelled word?"

*Estimate of Validity and Usefulness*

These are better tests than most. All five areas of emphasis listed above are important, but too few tests pay adequate attention to any of them except conventions (mechanical correctness). Many of the items are creatively structured. The degree of difficulty of items appears suitable to the designated grade levels. Use of student writings as points of take-off is much better than the use of concocted passages.

One weakness is that in one or two items in each test, more than a single answer could be reasonably defended. Another is that errors and infelicities in the student-written passages frequently go unmentioned. And, as is true of any writing that relies on indirect measurement, one cannot be sure that the person who scores high on this test will be a *good* writer; he or she is unlikely to be a very bad writer, yet proof of ability to edit someone else's writing does not necessarily prove that the test-taker can write well. Perhaps, indeed, as an earlier reviewer has suggested, the *STEP* Writing test is really a measure of general scholastic aptitude rather than of writing ability; its high correlations with tests designated as scholastic aptitude tests tend to support that belief.

The *Teacher's Guide* provides an unusual service: suggestions for using the test results to aid student learning. Class discussion of difficult items is recommended (most standardized tests are hush-hush; students take them and may never hear about them again). Also, the *Guide* suggests that classroom instruction can be geared to the needs of a specific class by examining the kinds of difficulty most common in the class. It suggests further *(mirabile dictu!)* that rewriting of the prose passages in the test provides a useful writing exercise. The *Guide* itself is well and interestingly written ("You may save yourself some time and fury if. . . ."), something seldom characteristic of test manuals.

# Literature Tests

*Alan C. Purves*

One of the most noticeable aspects of this section is the small number of tests available in literature despite its prominence in the school curriculum. The reasons for this phenomenon might include both the diversity in the curriculum and the intractability of the subject matter. Literature is avowedly not easy to make up tests about, as many of these tests demonstrate.

We have divided the tests into two groups: those dealing with the recall of information about selections already read (who wrote what? what character appears in what?) by the student, and those dealing with the student's understanding of works just read (usually with the text available to the student). The first kind of test suffers because of the transitory nature of many selections in the curriculum; most of the tests reviewed in this group need updating. A more serious problem is that of the diversity of offerings, even were all the selections current. *Macbeth* is taught in only 70 percent of the schools. What do we know of the pervasiveness of *My Name is Aram* or "Snowbound"? National tests of recall must then be reviewed carefully by a school and the results viewed within the context of the children's opportunity to learn *each* of the items on the test.

The second kind of test deals with reading ability and acumen, with comprehension and interpretation. As such, the test is similar to reading tests, save in the restriction of type of passage or selection. Many tests are carefully made and statistically sound. Their pitfalls include tendencies to deal only with low-level inferences (vocabulary, identification of speaker, and the like) and to try to force a single interpretation on the test-taker. An additional pitfall is neglect, in most of the tests reviewed, of the emotional and aesthetic aspects of our reading of literary works. Few questions deal with how students like a work, how it makes them feel, and what image it creates. Standardized tests like these, therefore, should not form the whole of an evaluation program. As a part of that program, these may be useful in varying degrees as the reviews show.

## Tests of Knowledge and Recall

**Stanford Achievement Test (SAT), High School Arts and Humanities Test**. Form X. Eric Gardner, Jack Merwin, Robert Callis, and Richard Madden. New York: Harcourt, Brace & World, 1965. (See Hook review p. 110 for *SAT* Primary Level II, Intermediate Level I, and Advanced Level Tests.)

Containing sixty-five four-choice items, the test covers literature, art, music, philosophy, and film. There is one passage for some analysis. The test is accompanied by an extensive manual describing the trials done in 1963 and the standardization done in 1965. The mean score for grade 9 was 29; grade 10, 32; grade 11, 36; and grade 12, 39. A college preparatory group scored somewhat higher.

*Evaluation*

This test requires students to recall biographical and historical information as well as factual information about artistic works and critical terms. Students are asked to identify such diverse items as van Eyck, Tanglewood, Taj Mahal, "numbers," and *The Catcher in the Rye*. Most of the items are clear and unambiguous, although they do not deal with much more than quiz show information. There is no real analysis or interpretation, no measurement of any real confrontation with an art work. Given this limitation and the one that no items deal with art by minority groups (save one item on Dixieland), the test is adequate.

**Hollingsworth-Sanders Junior High School Literature Test**. Test I, forms A and B; and Test II, forms A and B. Leon Hollingsworth and M. W. Sanders. Emporia, Kans.: Bureau of Educational Measurements, 1964.

There are four tests for grades 7 and 8, each with 105-150 four-choice questions. The tests rely on identification of quotations, characters, and titles. There is also a vocabulary section. The tests were normed in 1962 and 1963, using a national sample.

*Evaluation*

This test is now hopelessly inappropriate for its audience. It requires a recall of passages, titles, characters, authors, and incidents of works no longer taught or, if taught, not with any consistency in the junior high school. Often the works referred to are excerpts which are given nonce-titles in the texts. The authors base their tests upon "Homework," "Fast Ball," and "Mr. Chairman." Many of the items are ridiculous, "Sometimes we Americans refer to 1. Lord Byron, 2. Alfred Tennyson, 3. Edgar A. Poe, 4. William Shakespeare, 5. A. E. Housman as the master poet of all times." The quotations given are often obscure. There are no items dealing with works by minority group writers.

**Hoskins-Sanders Literature Tests.** Test I, forms A and B; Test II, forms A and B. Thomas Hoskins and M. W. Sanders. Emporia, Kans.: Bureau of Educational Measurements, 1964.

There are four 150-item, multiple-choice tests dealing with writers, titles, and literary terms; the tests are designed for grades 9-13. They cover British and American literature and give some attention to world literature. The authors claim that the test material deals with "35 classical selections." The tests were normed in 1963; the norms indicate that the 99th percentile at the 12th grade level averaged 90 out of 150 right.

*Evaluation*

As the norming data reveal, the series deals with details from a variety of literary works, both famous and trivial, measuring a student's recall of a large number of selections that were standard in the curriculum over a generation ago. The test ranges from Bede to Booth Tarkington and calls for knowledge of authors, titles, characters, events, and genres. It does measure breadth but in a hopelessly antiquated fashion. There is no reference to literature of minority groups and no attempt to measure analysis and interpretation.

**Iowa High School Content Examination for High School Seniors and College Freshmen**. Form L. G. M. Ruch, D. B. Stuit, and H. A. Greene. Iowa City: Bureau of Educational Research and Service, 1943.

As part of a several-subject test, there is a section of 100 four-choice items, mostly dealing with literature, although there are a number of items on usage and vocabulary. The test was normed in 1943 on samples of 11th and 12th grade students "scattered through the nation." The examination samples "important facts and concepts which a high school student could be expected to know upon completion of his high school course."

*Evaluation*

Without a doubt, this is one of the worst tests still in print. All of the items require recall of information. Most of the items are trivial (the authorship of *Mr. Britling Sees It Through*), unanswerable ("(1) Shakespeare (2) Pope (3) Eliot (4) Tennyson developed the idea of the immortality of the soul in his poems"), or fraught with mistakes (Scrooge's partner is referred to as Marlowe). The material is dated for high school students and there is no Black literature. The test does not measure the comprehension it purports to.

**Illinois Tests in the Teaching of English, Knowledge of Literature**. Competency test C. William H. Evans and Paul H. Jacobs. Carbondale, Ill.: Southern Illinois University Press, 1969 and 1972. (See Hook review p. 102 for Knowledge of Language test.)

The test, designed for prospective teachers, consists of 143 items, 121 of which ask the test-taker about literary works, periods, genres, and critical terms. The remainder deal with the critical reading of prose and poetry. Included in the identification and classification section are a number of works of juvenile and adolescent literature as well as Black literature and world literature. The test was tried out on prospective teachers, but there are no norming data.

### Evaluation

I had a chance to review many of the items for this test between try-out and final assembly of the test. Then as now, I was struck by the ingenuity of some of the item types, particularly the classification items, an example of which follows:

| 1. | | |
|---|---|---|
| | *Hamlet* | *A. Moby Dick* |
| | *Macbeth* | *B. The Scarlet Letter* |
| | *Romeo and Juliet* | *C. King Lear* |
| | | *D. Pride and Prejudice* |
| | | *E. David Copperfield* |

REASON: All were written by the same author.

The reasons extend over form, theme, authorship, period, and genre. In general, this part of the test measures a prospective teacher's knowledge of facts about books and authors well, although some items may already be dated. The critical reading section, although brief, is adequate, and the last set of items asking the test-taker to compare and contrast three poems about nature is well done. A person who does well on both parts of the test would certainly demonstrate a strong knowledge of literary facts and an ability to read with acumen. Whether there is more to literary study than those two abilities is another matter, but for its aims, this test succeeds.

**Literature Tests, Objective and Essay**. Fifty and 100 question series, and essay series. Logan, Iowa: The Perfection Form Co., 1946-1970.

Written by a variety of people, the objective series consists of 110 one-hundred-item tests and ninety fifty-item tests on some of "the greatest books ever written" (*Aeneid* to *The Yearling*). There are also essay tests on all 140 books. I have examined only those tests on *Lord of the Flies, The Bridge of San Luis Rey, Pygmalion, Moby Dick, The Red Badge of Courage, The Scarlet Letter, Treasure Island, Tom Sawyer, Silas Marner, The Return of the Native, The Odyssey, Oedipus Rex, Huckleberry Finn, The Old Man and the*

*Sea, Pride and Prejudice, Evangeline, Hamlet, The Human Comedy, Julius Caesar, Macbeth, Our Town, The Merchant of Venice,* and *Great Expectations.* The tests consist of true-false, matching, fill-in, and multiple-choice questions. There is no information on norms.

Since the tests are quite similar, I will describe the one on *Huckleberry Finn* (by N. F. Falk, 1950 and 1965) as typical. It contains five matching questions on the book, ten matching questions on character identification, twelve questions on animals and objects, thirty true-false questions, twenty-three multiple-choice questions, twelve short-answer questions, and eight completions. The items deal almost entirely with recall of details.

## Evaluation

The test violates most principles of test construction. The matching questions, for examples, contain equal numbers on both sides so that the test is one of elimination. The true-false questions contain matters of opinion (e.g., "Tom had an ingenious mind"). The fill-in questions presume a single answer to questions like, "Who tried to teach Huck?" Furthermore, the test deals with trivia. Does it matter that a banjo and a black shirt are objects that do not appear in the book? The test neglects any critical or thoughtful reading of the book. It forecloses all matters of controversy. The test on *Hamlet,* for instance, decides that it is true that Hamlet is not insane, a matter critics are still debating. Although the test might have some slight value to the teacher who wants to check on whether students have read these books, most teachers would do better with a five-minute, home-dittoed quiz. Schools which buy these tests would have no defense were a taxpayer's suit instituted charging the school with misappropriation of funds. The wastage would be not only one of money but of the time and energy of teachers and students.

## Tests of Critical Reading and Interpretation

**The NCTE Cooperative Test of Critical Reading and Appreciation, A Look at Literature**. Forms A and B. Roderick A. Ironside. Princeton, N.J.: Educational Testing Service, 1968.

There are two forms of this test, which is intended for fourth through sixth grade students. The forms are parallel, each containing fifty four-choice questions dealing with fourteen passages of prose and poetry. The authors have categorized the questions as dealing with translation, extension, and awareness (corresponding to comprehension, interpretation, and literary analysis). The two forms have been statistically equated and correlated with the *STEP* Reading test, and norms have been created based on a sample of some 500 students for each group. The test is designed primarily as a research instrument, although it can also be used as an instructional device and possibly as an evaluation device.

*Evaluation*

I took part in the initial item review for the test, so that some prejudice might be inferred. Nevertheless, the test does serve as an adequate measure of comprehension of literary texts. The selections are varied, including many classics of children's literature (Astrid Lindgreen, Laura Ingalls Wilder, Joseph Krumgold, and Robert Larson are among the authors represented). There is little ethnic or urban literature, however. The questions do range over a variety of abilities related to the reading of literature, and the choices represent the work of careful test construction and review. A weakness of the test is that not every passage is treated with the gamut of questions, so that the test-taker is faced with not particularly coherent sets of questions and therefore is not asked to synthesize his or her understanding. As an evaluation device, *A Look at Literature* must be supplemented with some other measures—essays or other written projects.

**Content Evaluation Series Language Arts Series, Literature Test.** Form I. Ruth Reeves (Kellogg W. Hunt, series editorial advisor). Boston: Houghton Mifflin Co., 1969. (See Hook review p. 103 for Language Ability test and Braddock review p. 122 for Composition test.)

The test, for use in grades 7-9, consists of forty-five four-choice items based on a reading of five passages: three poems, a selection of nonfiction, and one of drama. The questions deal with form and content. There was no norming information available.

*Evaluation*

Part of a series, this test measures the ability to read, analyze, and interpret literary selections. The test does measure higher mental processes, and it does follow the "new critical" line appropriate for objective measurement. Occasionally the items have overlong stems, thus making them answerable without recourse to the text, and occasionally the items are not of great significance to an understanding of the text. But nonetheless the test is sound. The test-makers are pretentious in claiming that the test measures a broad spectrum of abilities, but it is better than most in this respect. The situations used are a bit crusty and perhaps inappropriate to inner-city youth; there is no Black literature.

**Cooperative Literature Tests**. Forms A and B. Princeton, N.J.: Educational Testing Service, 1972.

This series of multiple-choice, open-book tests deals with selected major works of literature: *A Tale of Two Cities, The Old Man and the Sea, Julius Caesar, Macbeth, The Scarlet Letter, Silas Marner, Oedipus the King, The Bridge of San Luis Rey, Moby Dick, The Red Badge of Courage, Our Town, The Return of the Native, Pygmalion, The Merchant of Venice, Great Expectations, The Odyssey, Pride and Prejudice, Huckleberry Finn,* and *Hamlet.* For each work there are two tests, each of forty four-choice items. Although reliabilities and norms have been determined, they were not available at the time of review. The two tests may be used as a pretest and a post-test, or as a study test and a final test.

*Evaluation*

These are superbly printed tests, and their quality matches their covers. The items range over facts, character interpretations, style, form, theme, and mood of the works. To take *Pride and Prejudice* as an example, the test opens with disingenuous items:

"It is a truth universally acknowledged, that a single man in possession of a good fortune must be in want of a wife." All of the following statements accurately describe this first sentence of the

novel EXCEPT
1. It leads the reader on.
2. It establishes the ironic tone of the novel.
3. It says the reverse of what it means.
4. It states a profound and universal truth.

Although it is an easy question, answered in part by a knowledge of irony, and although it may be challenged by an item-writer, this item does set forth the *tone* of the test. It is serious, playful, and intellectual. The items that follow continue in this manner, with questions like, "In order for Elizabeth and Darcy to be brought together, it is necessary that. . . ."; "How does the elopement of Lydia and Wickham advance the plot?"; and "The characters chiefly attacked by the author's humor are those who. . . ." The students who take this test are challenged to read with care and discernment.

The virtue of two forms for each work is that of providing opportunities to measure growth. A fitting use would be to give one form at the beginning of an instructional unit, and to use the test to begin discussion. The second test could form part of a final evaluation. The two forms could also be used for action research. The forms are parallel without being redundant.

One might criticize these tests for being overly "new critical." But granted that perspective, the questions are excellently wrought. A more serious criticism is that of the order of items in the test. The questions seem arranged more in order of difficulty than according to the chronology of the work or to an order ranging from detail to generalization. Nonetheless, teachers could profitably use these tests either as unit tests or as springboards to essays and projects.

**Tests of Academic Progress, Literature**. Form S. Oscar M. Haugh and Dale P. Scannell. Boston: Houghton Mifflin Co., 1971. (See Hook review p. 113 for Composition test.)

The test contains 126 four-choice items based on a reading of passages of prose and poetry, including a passage from *Taming of the Shrew*. The test is printed so that the ninth grade does passages 1-5, tenth 3-7, eleventh 5-10, and twelfth 6-12; a teacher may thus compare grade levels. Items include vocabulary, comprehension, literary terms, and dating and geographical placement of the passages. Norming information was provided on norms of from 1113 to 1690, in Idaho and Montana, as well as a national sample. Norming data are given in terms of percentiles.

*Evaluation*

This test alternates between reading comprehension items and items of literary classification and interpretation. Often the former are not highly significant and the latter are of varying quality (for example, the identification of Shelley as the author of "Mutability" seems inappropriate). Some of the items rely on the students' having read the work before taking the test or knowing extraneous information. There is no coverage of materials by minority writers. There is no coherence to the sets of items for each passage so that the teacher cannot discriminate among lower and higher behaviors. As a test of the ability to analyze and interpret literary materials, this one is fair, but not of the best.

**Responding: Ginn Interrelated Sequences in Literature, Evaluation Sequence.** Pretests, growth tests, and diagnostic tests. Charles R. Cooper and Alan C. Purves. Lexington, Mass.: Ginn and Co., 1973.

[Review edited by Dan Donlan, University of California, Riverside.]

The *Evaluation Sequence* for Ginn's *Responding Series* is an intricate evaluation program based on a response grid which projects the interrelationships between, horizontally, eight student behaviors (creating, valuing, evaluating, generalizing, interpreting, relating, discriminating, and describing) and, vertically, two areas of content—the piece of literature itself (subject matter, voice, shape, and language) and the student's response to the piece of literature (spoken, written, and nonverbal). The five types of measures comprising the evaluation program, placed on the response grid where the authors deem appropriate, assess the program's objectives: (1) Attitude Scales help in evaluating what students value in literature and how they describe their responses; (2) Diagnostic Tests of Specific Skills (grades 7-12), focusing on seven areas of literary understanding (e.g., perceiving character traits, perceiving tone and mood), indicate student abilities in interpreting and discriminating; (3) Pretests and (4) Growth Tests (both grades 7-12), each containing thirty-six multiple-choice items on literature excerpts, hopefully unfamiliar to the student, assess student abilities in interpreting, relating, and discriminating; and (5) Teacher-made Questionnaires, including inventories in student interest and class climate, supplement other instruments and provide information not assessable elsewhere. The authors indicate openly the areas the *Evaluation Sequence* does not measure. *A Guide to Evaluation* is the evaluator's handbook, containing not only pertinent information on uses of the various instruments, but also samples for teacher-designed instruments and helpful essays on literary criticism, the nature of response, and devices for evaluating response.

## Evaluation

One can only be impressed by the thoroughness of the Cooper-Purves evaluation program, which attempts to assess, in a variety of ways, both the emotional and intellectual responses of students. The *Evaluation Sequence* is tightly, logically generated, first from five stated assumptions about literary response, second from a response grid, and third from a series of general and specific, verifiable objectives. In fact, one might argue that *A Guide to Evaluation* is a textbook on student response, and, herein may be the program's principal problem.

As with many theoretical documents which supply specific examples to illustrate theory, teachers may "snatch up" this or that without understanding the underlying assumptions of student response, ultimately defeating the purpose of the theory. The authors devoutly and repeatedly caution teachers about the use of the various instruments. For instance, they emphasize the diagnosis of growth and deemphasize grading. Yet, I wonder if many teachers will not assign letter grades to each evaluative experience. In some multiple-choice tests, a fifth option permits the student to write in his or her own choice. Despite the authors' explanations, I wonder how many teachers will take the time to deal with variances from "the key," or, for that matter, to implement the ingeniously designed "attitude sort," the "class climate inventory," and the forms dealing with observation and description of responses. In effect, teachers using Ginn's *Responding Series* need a developmental, articulate inservice program to deal with the subtlety, richness, and complexity of transactive response. In other words, there's beauty in the Cooper-Purves program, but it's not there for the mere taking.

3

# Problems and Recommendations

*Alfred H. Grommon*

In Part Two of this report, reviews of many different standardized tests have pointed to specific problems that English teachers face as they attempt to reconcile the demands of standardized tests with the attitudes and skills that are taught in their classrooms. To broaden the perspective, consider the four general kinds of problems detailed by Henry S. Dyer in the 1971 speech cited earlier, "The State Assessment Survey."

One problem has to do with lack of communication among various groups within a state that may be working independently on trying to devise some sort of assessment program. . . . This lack of communication is likely to become a breeder of conflict and confusion, and the conflict and confusion threaten to neutralize the whole effort. . . .

A second problem that is beginning to crop up in those situations where statewide testing programs are under consideration has to do with the manner in which the results will be used in the allocation of state funds to local school districts. . . .

A third problem is the well-known one of how to protect the confidentiality of the information being gathered in the assessment process—especially when this information includes data supplied by pupils about the economic and social conditions of their families. The mere fact that such information is being gathered at all—regardless of efforts to guard the anonymity of the children who supply it—tends to generate storms in parent groups and state legislatures. And these storms are often exacerbated by headlines in the local press.

Finally, in connection with the efforts to formulate meaningful educational goals around which to build an assessment program, there is the perennial problem of confusion between ends and

141

means, between process and product, between pupil performance objectives, staff performance objectives, and institutional performance objectives, between management by objectives and management by prescription. . . . Until we can find some better methods than we now have of getting people unconfused in this matter of goals and objectives, such assessment programs as may eventuate in the next few years are not likely to have much substantive impact on the improvement of education in any state.[1]

## What Teachers Can Do

The 1973 Educational Testing Service surveys reveal that in many states administrators and teachers already are well aware of the problems mentioned above and are striving to resolve or at least reduce them. Nevertheless, concerned teachers, in the interest of being informed about the testing programs in their state and of improving communication among involved groups should obtain the following kinds of information:

— copies of the state's laws in which educational accountability is mandated;
— other materials showing the schematic design of the state's system of educational accountability;
— copies of the state's educational goals;
— any documents containing results of appraisals of the state's program of testing and assessment;
— information about the creation and use of criterion-referenced tests;
— reports of how the results of achievement tests are used as a basis for educational decisions for the state and for local school districts;
— information about what the state is doing to help local school districts develop their own programs of accountability.

These kinds of information should be available in every state. The better informed teachers are, the more effective their communication with other groups involved in the programs, including parents. The more significant their participation in the program, the less likely they are to play the role of being merely one of its agents, or its victims.

Though problems in selecting and using standardized tests and then interpreting and disseminating results may be plentiful and perplexing, some of the encouraging trends in aspects of statewide programs of testing identified earlier and adaptations of some of the following recommendations may help teachers of English anticipate some difficulties, minimize the effects of others, and in general enhance the status of their roles in the programs. As has been pointed out already, failure in communication among participants and those affected by testing programs is a major local and national problem. Whatever else may be the focus of each of the following recommendations, each is intended also to suggest or imply better communication among persons concerned about the uses of tests.

### Recommendation One: English teachers should participate in decisions about testing.

English teachers should participate in whatever groups are appointed to make education decisions about statewide and local programs of educational testing. They should be involved in identifying goals, in selecting and creating tests, in interpreting test results, in placing those results in the context of the entire English program, in furthering communication among various groups—state education officers and agencies, local administrators, teachers, students, parents, news media, other lay citizens—and in disseminating test results and interpretations to educational authorities, students, parents, and the local public in general.

### Recommendation Two: English teachers should publicize professional standards.

In contributing to planning sessions involving programs of educational accountability, English teachers should bring to the attention of all involved the 1971 resolutions on educational accountability and behavioral objectives that were issued by the National Council of Teachers of English. These resolutions testify to English teachers' recognition of their responsibility to be accountable to students, colleagues, parents, the local community, and to the wider community. But the resolution on accountability also emphasizes that each of these other groups has to be held accountable, in turn, to teachers.

### Recommendation Three: English teachers must help to interpret test validity.

There is often an assumption, sometimes faulty, that the results of students' performance on standardized tests are necessarily directly related to the quality of instruction they received on the particular subject matter of the test. As was reported earlier, the most common purpose in statewide programs of testing and assessment is to use test results to evaluate programs and instruction. Consequently, English teachers find themselves enmeshed in this kind of application of standardized test results. In such a case, teachers may be able to draw upon some of the following materials in interpreting test results for outside agencies and the public.

Chauncey and Dobbins of the Educational Testing Service raise the basic question: "Should tests be used to assess teachers?" In discussing this question, they point out some complications and implications of using the results of pupils' performances on standardized achievement tests for the purpose of judging the effectiveness of their teachers. They state, in part, that:

> Administrators, either on their own or at the insistence of parents and school board members, all too often judge the quality of a teacher's instruction by the average scores earned by the teacher's students on a standardized test. This can be far more dangerous than even the most knowledgeable advocates of educational measurement are likely to know. The danger lies in the fact that it is so easy to accept test results as the only evidence of teaching quality—when at their best, tests can yield only a small part of the evidence necessary to make a sound judgment. . . .
>
> The same considerations as those used with regard to judging the effectiveness of school systems must be made in assessing the individual teacher. Do the tests measure an important part of what the teacher is trying to teach? Does the teacher recognize that they do? Is it known exactly what kinds of pupils the teacher has to teach, his "raw material"? Are there provisions for before-and-after assessment, so that his effectiveness will be judged by the changes he produces? Is the teacher a member of the assessment team, rather than its victim? Unless these critical questions can all be answered in the affirmative, the teacher of bright and academically favored students will be far more effective than the teacher of the less-favored children, whose very real achievements will not be evident.[2]

They go on to say later that "standardized tests of student achievement are such useful teaching tools that it is often a mistake to try to make them do double duty as measures of the teacher as well."

Further complications of any relation between test outcomes and a teacher's effectiveness in working with "raw material" are pointed

out by Ned A. Flanders in his article, "The Changing Base of Performance-Based Testing." He says that the current problem in measuring educational outcomes is that "most of the tests used to measure
student learning appear to be insensitive to differences in teaching
behavior." One might add they seem to be insensitive also to differences in pupils' cognitive styles. Later in his article, Flanders states:

> One difficulty with measures of learning outcomes has been an
> over-emphasis on the subject matter achievement of students.
> There are two aspects of this problem. First, using a test of sub-
> ject matter as the only criterion of learning is inadequate, because
> student learning includes much more. For example, one might
> nominate staying in school and not dropping out; learning to like
> schooling, the process of learning, and the teacher, in contrast
> with hating them; gradually learning how to be more self-direct-
> ing and independent; learning how to make moral and ethical
> judgments. Any of these may be more important measures of
> teaching than are scores on reading, writing, and arithmetic.
> *Second, given the common focus on a subject matter and a re-*
> *search design consisting of a pretest, teaching/learning, and post-*
> *test, it was soon discovered that posttest achievement is at least 10*
> *times more strongly associated with pretest scores than it is with*
> *any measure of teaching. . . . Another problem is that standard-*
> *ized achievement tests are designed to be insensitive to the influ-*
> *ence of a particular teacher and reflect, instead, the total develop-*
> *ment background of the student. . . .* In spite of these difficulties,
> it *is* possible to analyze teaching effectiveness, but it will require
> some rethinking, some innovations, and some retooling with re-
> spect to the criterion measure.[3]

Lee J. Cronbach said something particularly relevant here: "Different children learn different things from training."[4]

Teachers finding themselves evaluated on the basis of their pupils'
performances on standardized tests in English may well find, in the
preceding statements, leads for helping others see the limitations
and dangers of drawing such inferences from test results. Such
teachers may identify also such evidence as Flanders points out
about teachers' and schools' influences upon perhaps more important outcomes of pupils' learning.

One account of a teacher's experiences in these matters may touch
directly some experiences of English teachers and may evoke a wry
smile of recognition. In the research leading to his report, *Deciding*

*the Future*, Edmund J. Farrell received the following letter from an English teacher on his panel of informants:

> My own research has convinced me that red-inking errors in students' papers does no good and causes a great many students to hate and fear writing more than anything else they do in school. I gave a long series of tests covering 580 of the most common and persistent errors in usage, diction, and punctuation and 1,000 spelling errors to students in grades 9-12 in many schools, and the average rate of improvement in ability to detect these errors turned out to be 2 per cent per year. The dropout rate is more then enough to account for this much improvement if the teachers had not even been there. When I consider how many hours of my life I have wasted in trying to root out these errors by a method that clearly did not work, I want to kick myself. Any rat that persisted in pressing the wrong lever 10,000 times would be regarded as stupid. I must have gone on pressing it at least 20,000 times without visible effect.[5]

The number of teachers of English pushing wrong levers is probably incalculable.

On the relation of test data to caliber of instruction, a statement quoted earlier from the ETS survey of statewide assessments seems appropriate here too: "It is probably safe to say that statewide assessment will not produce any startling revelations about what can be done by teachers with pupils to help children learn more effectively." Though standardized tests, appropriately selected and used, can be helpful aids in teaching and evaluation, any attempt to use the results of such tests, as single measures, as means also for assessing teachers can be seriously misleading.

**Recommendation Four: English teachers should demand an appropriate relationship between standardized tests and the purposes of the entire English program.**

Teachers of English should insist that whatever standardized tests may be used are, at the outset, appropriately related to the purposes and nature of their entire English program. They should strive also to make sure the public, educational authorities, and the news media see that relationship clearly.

A memorandum, "Specifications for Evaluation Strategy," prepared by teachers of English in the Bellevue, Washington, Public

Schools illustrates what the teachers did to present the essentials of their English program and, at the same time, provide a guide for test-development agencies interested in responding to the "need for an instrument and strategies to evaluate the program of *English Language Arts and Skills in the Bellevue Public Schools.*" The memorandum included the following statements:

1. Purposes for an Evaluation Program
2. Specifications for an Evaluative Instrument and Strategies
3. Assumptions about the English Program
4. Experiences ("The Developmental Expectations") provided for students in our program, K - 12
5. Short Term Outcomes that students might be expected to demonstrate after the experience-expectations have been provided[6]

It would appear that any evaluative instrument designed to fulfill these detailed specifications would have to be in keeping with the explicit purposes of that English program: its objectives, content, skills, and cognitive and affective experiences provided for students in Bellevue English classes. Such a product created to meet these requirements would be different indeed from commercially prepared, norm-referenced standardized English tests readily available from publishers and intended to be usable in any school, no matter what the special features of that community or its English program.

Another example of a statewide project designed to help teachers of English throughout Wisconsin is reported in the pamphlet, *Evaluation of Published English Tests,* prepared as a "guide for administrators, supervisors and teachers of English in the selection and use of standardized tests." The pamphlet presents evaluations of sixteen commercially prepared tests that seemed in 1966 to be the most frequently used by English teachers throughout Wisconsin to assess pupils' skills in aspects of spelling, vocabulary, sentence structure, awareness of elements of grammar, and conventions of written English.[7] In response to questionnaires, teachers who were experienced in using particular tests in their classes wrote evaluations of these tests. To the summaries of teachers' evaluations were added summaries of reviews published in *The Fifth Mental Measurements Yearbook* and *The Sixth Mental Measurements Yearbook,*[8] and also the occasional review in a professional journal. In the conclusions and recommendations, Wood lists questions teachers and school districts ought to answer satisfactorily before selecting and using a standardized test:

1. What portions of the content of English at the grade levels to be tested are included in this test?
2. Is this proportionate emphasis parallel to the emphasis given by our teachers?
3. Does this test measure what our teachers consider to be a basic part of their curriculum? In other words, does it truly test our curriculum?
4. Are the presented items valid? For example, are the items of usage, punctuation, sentence corrections, and other details consistent with what we teach?
5. What is the time required for this test?
6. How easy is it to administer? Are the directions simple and clear?
7. How easily may the test be scored?
8. What do the scores mean when completed?
9. How are the norms derived? How extensive was the sampling?
10. How can the results of this test be followed up for the improvement of the English program?[9]

Today, any teacher of English or school district about to engage in a testing program undoubtedly would ask additional questions representing priorities apparently not raised by Wisconsin English teachers during the 1960s. Nevertheless, the questions are sensible, practical, useful, and still highly relevant to any consideration of standardized tests in English.

Still another example of a statewide project is the use of the *English Language Framework for California Public Schools, Kindergarten through Grade Twelve* (California State Department of Education, 1968) during 1972-74 as the basis for the preparation of guidelines for designing English tests to be used in compliance with a state law. This *Framework* was prepared by the California Advisory Committee for an English Framework comprised of teachers, supervisors, and college and university professors of English and Education working in conjunction with thousands of English teachers and supervisors throughout the state. The *Framework* was adopted by the State Department of Education in 1968 and again in 1971. During 1974, it was revised by a statewide committee of teachers of English and of English educators. Long though this process has been, the Advisory Committee, nevertheless, thereby achieved a high degree of communication statewide among English teachers, administrators, college and university professors, and the State Department of Education. Testimony to these benefits appeared in subsequent developments.

In 1972, the California State Legislature, insisting upon holding public schools accountable to the state and public, adopted a law stipulating that in 1974-1975 a continuing program of statewide testing on the basis of matrix sampling would be instituted in the sixth and twelfth grades. This program was to measure the effectiveness of pupils' written expression and their abilities in spelling. As a crucial first step in involving English teachers and school districts in helping the State Department of Education evolve the best possible English tests to be administered in compliance with this law, the State Office of Program Evaluation and Research invited representative school and college teachers of English to serve as an English Language Assessment Advisory Committee.

The Advisory Committee worked two years in preparing its report, *Guidelines for Designing Tests to be Used to Assess 6th- and 12th-Grade Students' Competencies in Written Expression and Spelling*. The opening paragraphs illustrate the intent of the Advisory Committee to ensure that whatever tests were developed must be in keeping with the state Framework and the principles underlying the entire guidelines:

Any California program of State-wide assessment of public school pupils' competencies related to their command of the English language should be founded upon certain principles presented in three documents:

1. the *English Language Framework for California Public Schools* (adopted in 1968; readopted in 1971);
2. the "Criteria for Evaluating Instructional Materials for English and Related Studies, K-8," prepared by the English Advisory Group of the California State Curriculum Commission, published in the *CATE Bulletin*, Spring, 1971;
3. recommendations by the English Language Assessment Advisory Committee (1972-73).

The following principles, drawn from the above sources, are intended to serve as guidelines for the California State Department of Education Office of Program Evaluation and Research, for any publishers of standardized tests interested in this State-wide program in evaluation, and for representatives of the schools that will be using tests developed to fulfill stipulations of the Greene Bill and will be discussing this program of evaluation in their communities.

Although the tests to be administered in compliance with the Greene Bill will be designed to assess pupils' competence in using the English language effectively and in spelling, these separate tests should also reflect the developers' awareness of the definition of English as a school subject and of the principle of unity and sequence of English programs as recommended throughout the *English Language Framework*. The definition of English is implied throughout the *Framework*, but the following is a direct statement of purposes of such a program:

> The chief aims of the school program in English are, as the Curriculum Commission has stated, to develop in all children who graduate from the twelfth grade . . . competence in listening, speaking, reading, and writing English and as much appreciation and understanding as possible of the literature of America, England, and the world.

To reinforce the Advisory Committee's stand that any English tests used in compliance with this law must be consistent with the *English Language Framework*, the delegates to the annual meeting of the California Association of Teachers of English, in February 1973, passed a resolution calling for an amendment to the State Education Code to make sure that the law specified this relationship: ". . . to require that statewide tests in English (language, literature, reading, and writing) reflect accurately the principles set forth in the *English Language Framework for California Public Schools*. . . ." This resolution was then forwarded to the state legislature.

In May 1974, the State Department of Education sent to publishers the *Guidelines*, including objectives, specifications, and sample test items. In the same month, the document was sent to 200 California school districts for their review and comment. In addition, as a means of continuing and improving communication, the state office periodically prepares and distributes a leaflet entitled "FEEDBACK, Newsletter of the New California English Testing Program."

The above was an example of how one state department of education drew upon many English teachers throughout the state to make sure the tests used were of the best possible kind. The California story is detailed here, and in Recommendation Seven, in order to suggest to English teachers and administrators in other states what may be done to improve the quality of statewide testing. In summary, it should be pointed out again that through the initiative of the California State Department of Education in establishing an Advisory Committee and through the full, congenial cooperation of its representative working with the group, the Committee was able to draw to the attention of the State Department, the school districts throughout the state, and the interested publishers of tests the necessity of placing any statewide testing in English clearly within the context of the whole program of English as represented in the *English Language Framework for California Public Schools.*

**Recommendation Five: English teachers should insure the confidentiality of test results.**

As has been indicated earlier, reporting to the public the results of students' performances on standardized tests may sometimes pose problems of confidentiality, particularly those that may encroach upon the privacy of the individual pupil and perhaps adversely affect a sense of self-worth. Most statewide programs are designed to yield information about the quality of pupils' performances on the basis of results for a school, district, or state. Tests are intended to help evaluate programs, not individuals. To minimize these difficulties and, in some ways, simplify statewide testing, several states have designed programs of testing on the basis of matrix sampling, a pattern ensuring that no pupil gets the entire test. Rather, each gets a certain sampling of all items comprising the entire test. The various samplings distributed in a school or district, however, do constitute the entire test. As a result of such a sampling pattern, the level of performance of pupils as a group, in a program or district, can be measured; however, the evidence of how an individual pupil might perform on the entire test is not available. The use of some pattern of sampling is one of the recommendations made by the Michigan panel of educators who assessed that state's program of accountability. Yet in other kinds of local testing programs in which teachers wish to know how well individual pupils are performing on a test of particular aspects of an English program, they can select or create a different kind of measurement. The feedback of test results can enable teachers to help the individual pupil and to re-examine the English program. Whatever the nature of the instruments, of the administration of the tests, and of the handling of results, all must be treated with care to protect the individual pupil's sense of self-worth.

**Recommendation Six: English teachers should maintain vigilance of test validity.**

Teachers should continue to examine what they consider to be the validity of the content of standardized English tests already a part of a continuing program of assessment and of other tests available to them for their own purposes.

The following guidelines developed by the aforementioned California English Language Assessment Advisory Committee may help other English teachers in evaluating both the content and format of standardized English tests they are now using or are considering for possible use:

The Committee also recommends the following guidelines representing specific application of the preceding principles as further aids for whoever will be responsible for developing a valid test of competencies in the uses of English in accordance with the Greene Bill:

1. Test items should reflect an awareness that a child's initial development of language competence is in the dialect or language acquired within his linguistic environment. Although it may not be possible to construct *culture free* tests, considerable effort should be devoted to developing tests that are *culturally fair.*

2. Questions requiring pupils to discriminate among choices of usage and diction should be based upon the criteria of what is appropriate to a speaker, his audience, and the situation in which the usage is to be uttered rather than upon any traditional concept of so-called "correctness" in the use of the English language in the abstract.

3. Accordingly, questions related to usage should specify the speaker and the situation in which these items of usage are to be considered, thereby indicating the relationship between the speaker, the audience, and the context in which the individual is speaking.

4. Test items related to questions of English usage should also reflect the principle that informal English is appropriate in many contexts.

5. Questions related to appropriateness of usage and diction should be intended further to encourage pupils and teachers to accept the natural and simple use of the English language rather than the pedantic and the awkward.

6. Settings in which the language items are being used and the items in questions should be appropriate to the maturity levels and interests of students being tested. For example, items testing pupils' vocabulary and command of syntax should be appropriate to the grade level being tested.

7. Many items should be written at a level of difficulty in reading below that at which students are being tested.

8. Items should represent the range of practical and academic applications of the use of the English language that students face.

9. Items should not include specific grammatical terminology unless the meaning of such terms is easily discernible in the context of the item or is directly defined.

10. The basic recommendation on the format of any test is that subtests should be designated as single sample with all test items derived from the example. All items within a subtest should be related to a sample situation or setting, thereby maintaining the unified or holistic nature of the language arts. Meaning is frequently derived more from context than from single words, phrases, and sentences; to test for any concept of effective written expression out of context can seem confusing and unreal. The sample itself may be a letter, paragraph, editorial, news story, or even dictionary entry so long as it provides a range of possible questions on effective expression and is in itself free of gross errors.

11. Grouping and Format of Items:
    In each subtest similar test items should be arranged together so that the student taking the test can focus on sentence patterns, sentence manipulation, punctuation, diction, and all other test elements one at a time. The physical layout of the single sample ideally would have the sample presented once as an uninterrupted piece; for examination purposes the sample could appear as the left-hand column and the test items as the right-hand column on the same page. Items may be of the true-false or multiple choice varieties with preference for the latter.

Almost all standardized tests related to pupils' command of the English language include items based upon the testmakers' concept of what is acceptable usage and diction. At least seven of the above guidelines alert testmakers and teachers to the complexities and subtleties of language usage and to the difficulty of trying to test this phenomenon. The principles in the guidelines may help in appraising the content and format of standardized tests or may suggest other features closely related to the teacher's individual circumstance.

The following resolution, *Students' Right to Their Own Language*, adopted by the Executive Committee of the NCTE Conference on College Composition and Communication in March

1972, and approved at the official business meeting of the CCCC in April 1974, may serve also to remind teachers of the desirability of having an open attitude toward language usage, particularly that of pupils, and may offer them a reinforced criterion for judging whether or not the current status of language arts is adequately reflected in standardized English tests:

> We affirm the students' right to their own patterns and varieties of language—the dialects of their nurture or whatever dialects in which they find their own identity and style. Language scholars long ago denied that the myth of a standard American dialect has any validity. The claim that any one dialect is unacceptable amounts to an attempt of one social group to exert its dominance over another. Such a claim leads to false advice for speakers and writers, and immoral advice for humans. A nation proud of its diverse heritage and its cultural and racial variety will preserve its heritage of dialects. We affirm strongly that teachers must have the experiences and training that will enable them to respect diversity and uphold the right of students to their own language.[10]

Although such a position statement may be unsettling to some teachers, it should incline them, nevertheless, to reconsider carefully the nature of their own attitudes toward diversity in language. They might examine also some implications not only for their treatment of language in their classes and in their relationships with individual pupils but also for the nature of the standardized English tests that they favor.

**Recommendation Seven: English teachers should seek the support of professional associations.**

Teachers dissatisfied with English tests now in use in their schools need not despair in silence. The NCTE and its affiliates often pass resolutions stating teachers' strong convictions about kinds and uses of tests. Some of these resolutions are quoted or referred to in this discussion. The continuing account of activities in California illustrates what English teachers can do about these problems. In 1971 the California Association of Teachers of English (CATE), a state affiliate of NCTE, approved a resolution growing out of widespread disapproval of the statewide use of a standardized test selected by the State Board of Education. The test was used to comply with requirements established by the California State Legislature in 1968, whereby achievement testing in basic skills courses became mandatory. Some members of CATE made a detailed, highly critical analysis of the English test then being used and published part of their report in the "CATE Curriculum Newsletter," (Spring 1971). Some high school English Departments also spoke out against the test and its use in California. These and other protests culminated in the following CATE resolution published in the same newsletter: "RESOLVED That the California Association of Teachers of English urge the California State Board of Education to abandon further use of the Iowa Tests of Educational Development, Form X-4, Test 3, Correctness and Appropriateness of Expression, and declare the results of the tests for 1969 and 1970 as meaningless for the State of California." Whatever the consequence of this action may have been, the California State Department of Education appointed, one year later, the English Language Assessment Advisory Committee that wrote the *Guidelines.* Following the *Guidelines,* the State Office of Program Evaluation and Research took the initial steps in developing a tailor-made test of the effectiveness of written expression and spelling to be used first in 1974-75.

### Recommendation Eight:  English teachers should consider creating tailor-made tests.

As already mentioned, the ETS surveys of statewide programs report that several states are using, and others are in the process of creating, tests tailored to fit their educational goals, programs, and other circumstances. Many tailor-made tests also are designed to help pupils and teachers identify some noncognitive elements of their educational experiences. As indicated earlier, an increasing number of states are, or will be, using criterion-referenced test instruments. For example, in the ETS survey of assessment (p. 42), Michigan reported that its State Department of Education was coordinating a project involving cooperation between the California Test Bureau-McGraw-Hill, Inc., and four local Michigan school districts in developing criterion-referenced tests based upon state specifications. These tests were to be used in the 1973 administration of the assessment program.[11]

Because most, if not all, teachers who create their own class tests are already designing some form of criterion-referenced examinations, they may wish to consult some aids on the development and use of such tests. One helpful reference is Robert B. Carruthers' pamphlet, "Building Better English Tests, A Guide for Teachers of English in Secondary Schools."[12] In it, Carruthers analyzes and illustrates fundamental topics such as planning the test, basic characteristics of effective tests and test questions, selecting proper test questions, building effective short-answer items and essay questions, and reviewing the results of the test.

A criterion-referenced test offers the advantage of being suited to local circumstances and limited to a small segment of a course or program. But problems inhere also in judging the results of a pupil's performance. For instance, how many correct answers must a pupil make before a particular objective is considered achieved? If the test is applied to a program rather than to a unit in a particular course, at what grade level is he or she expected to be able to meet particular objectives? Do the objectives apply to all pupils in that grade?[13] Designers and local users of criterion-referenced tests have to answer these and other questions in making educational decisions involving the selection and use of tests and their results.

In considering uses of tailor-made and standardized tests, English teachers may wish to give special attention to the use of tests as a means of exploring pupils' experiences with literature. As will be seen in the reviews of standardized tests of literature presented earlier, the tests may place a premium upon a pupil's memorized knowledge of aspects of literature rather than upon ascertaining the nature and range of the students' responses to a literary selection or to a variety of selections in a unit. In other words, how can a teacher attempt to ascertain some aspects of a student's *affective* experiences with literature? Some help on these subtle but basic qualities in a reader's responses may be found in the Carruthers' pamphlet; however, more extensive information may be obtained from Purves' and Beach's *Literature and the Reader: Research in Response to Literature, Reading Interests, and the Teaching of Literature.*[14]

A list prepared by the Dallas, Texas, Independent School System could serve as an additional guide for teachers and schools interested in creating and using criterion-referenced tests.[15] The following is this author's version of the list, edited to suit the purposes here:

1. A criterion-referenced test (CRT) evaluates what a student knows or does not know. The student is evaluated against the objective, not against national norms or the achievements of other students.

2. CRT's are based upon a set of specified instructional objectives which describe the developmental instruction program. These objectives identify the act, define the conditions under

which it is to occur, and often describe the standard of acceptable performance.

3. The use of criterion-referenced tests should tend to make educational objectives apparent and provide information about what the individual student can or cannot do.

4. Measurement of achievement can be defined as the assessment of terminal criterion behavior: a student's performance with respect to specified standards.

5. Achievement measurement is directed toward a student's present performance; whereas, aptitude is related to both present performance and prospects of future attainment.

6. Minimum levels of performance need to be specified in behavioral terms and to describe the least amount of competence the student is expected to attain at the end of the instruction-learning. Information about conditions or instructional treatments also can be provided.

7. Criterion-referenced tests are developed to determine the relationship between a student's performance and objectives of teaching-learning. Because the tests are not normed, the usual reporting of results in reference to a population based upon a "normal curve" is not relevant. Results are usually reported instead in terms of the percentage of students mastering the objective.

8. Criteria for "acceptable" performance can be established by comparing the performance of students with those of other students and by developing absolute standards of excellence.

9. Pre-testing is important because the criterion of behavior at the end of instruction alone does not dictate methods of teaching, but differences between a student's behavior before and after instruction do.

10. CRT's are devised to help make decisions about individuals and educational treatments.

11. Variability in performances is irrelevant in analyzing results of a CRT. The significance of a performance is not dependent upon comparisons with scores made by others.

12. The chief factor in the construction of a CRT is that each item is an accurate reflection of a criterion behavior.

13. A CRT may result in each participant's getting a perfect score. Thus, the typical index of internal consistency (split half) is not appropriate for a CRT.

14. Procedures for examining validity of content are more suited to CRT's.

15. In a CRT, an item that doesn't discriminate among responses need not be eliminated from the test if it reflects an important attribute of the criterion.

16. When decisions are to be made on a number of individuals and comparisons of individuals are necessary, NRT's are used. But when individualized instruction increases and information about competencies an individual has or does not have is needed, CRT's are used.

17. In constructing a CRT, one should consider the extent of the discipline to be measured, the number of objectives to be covered, the number of items for each objective, the method of scoring, the amount of time required for administering the test, and the manner in which test results are to be registered. A CRT must have relevance, objectivity, and specificity. Indices of difficulty and discrimination should be homogeneous.

Teachers in states not already using criterion-referenced tests may wish to obtain samples of some now available elsewhere.[16] These may prove to be useful models, a guide for teachers interested in fashioning their own versions. The models offered by Carruthers may help English teachers improve their measurement of their students' achievement at the end of a unit or course. Such ventures might be especially worthwhile for those who find little connection between their students' classroom achievement and the results of standardized, norm-referenced tests.

**Recommendation Nine: English teachers should be sure tests are administered properly.**

The ETS surveys report that in almost all instances it is the classroom teacher who administers tests to students. No doubt the states provide each teacher with explicit instructions on exactly how the tests are to be administered. Nevertheless, the checklist below, from the Dallas, Texas, Independent School System, offers helpful reminders to any teacher administering any sort of test:[17]

|  |  | Yes | No |
|---|---|---|---|
| 1. | Were the students allowed to use the restrooms before testing? | — | — |
| 2. | Was there a testing sign on the room door? | — | — |
| 3. | Were any students excluded from testing before or during the test by the teacher? | — | — |

4. Did any of the students refuse to take the test?      — —

5. Was there a sufficient amount of testing materials and pencils?      — —

6. Were the appropriate marking techniques demonstrated to the students?      — —

7. Were the students shown how to cross out a mark completely if they wished to change their answer to a particular question?      — —

8. Did the administrator attempt to create a relaxed atmosphere indicating that he expected each student to do his best?      — —

9. Were sample items explained, if there were any sample items?      — —

10. During the demonstration of a sample item, was the test booklet held on a level with the students' eyes as they were seated?      — —

11. Were all the students able to see the teacher from where they were working?      — —

12. Were seating arrangements made to discourage cheating?      — —

13. After the explanation of the sample item, were the students asked if they had any questions?      — —

14. Were the directions repeated for any of the sample items?      — —

15. Were the directions repeated for any of the scored items?      — —

16. Were directions given in a clear, natural, and pleasant voice?      — —

17. Were the test instructions read verbatim from the test manual?      — —

18. Were any personal assistance or hints given to any of the students on test items?      — —

19. Were the students constantly checked to ensure they were working on the correct page and item?      — —

20. Were markers used by the students to help them keep their place?      — —

21. Were there any interruptions during the administration of the test? If yes, how many?      — —

22. Were the testing sessions scheduled as recommended by the test manual?      — —

23.  Were any of the time limits set for individual tests or items altered?    — —
24.  Was a brief rest period provided between two tests or test sessions?    — —
25.  Was the classroom atmosphere relaxed during testing?    — —
26.  Were students talking during the testing session?    — —
27.  Was the testing stopped at the appropriate time?    — —
28.  Did the teacher seem to have control over the entire testing situation?    — —
29.  Were irregularities recorded and sent with test materials for scoring?    — —
30.  Were efforts made to insure that all students understood the instructions?    — —
31.  Did the test administrator paraphrase or present anything new to the standardized instructions?    — —
32.  If questions were asked relative to "guessing," did the administrator reread the instructions which refer to guessing or inform students to "do the best you can" if there were not instructions on guessing?    — —
33.  If the administrator used a timer, did he keep up with the regular time and mark the regular time down as a backup device?    — —
34.  Was overtesting avoided during a single day to avoid anxiety and boredom?    — —

**Recommendation Ten:  English teachers should be sure tests are not dehumanizing.**

A final reminder here is that all tests are designed for and administered to human beings. Permeating English teachers' comments about standardized tests is their concern lest the use of such instruments and the corollary antecedent—quantifiable behavioral objectives—should lead to dehumanizing of English as a school subject and to giving pupils the impression of being treated mechanistically. Undoubtedly, all English teachers consider themselves guardians of the humanistic tradition in life, in general, and in education, in particular. The uses of tests and this genuine uneasiness of English teachers need not be antagonistic. Trends discussed earlier suggest a growing compatibility between some forms of testing and the larger goals of a subject like English: notably, the establishing of statewide goals recognizing cognitive and noncognitive outcomes of education; the increased use of assessment to identify affective aspects of pupils' educational experiences; and increased use of criterion-referenced and other tests tailored to fit school and nonschool circumstances of an individual or of a particular group of pupils.

The following list, also from the Dallas school system,[18] seems in keeping with English teachers' concern with the child as a person and offers wholesome reminders to anyone using any kind of test:

1. Every pupil has a worth that is not measured by any test.
2. It is for the good of the student that tests are administered.
3. Test results must be supplemented by factors such as the following:
    (1) *student factors*—motivation, aspirations, temporary and permanent health, home environment, and previous school environment;
    (2) *school factors*—curriculum, textbooks used, teaching material and supplies, general adequacy of school plant and equipment, type and extent of supervision, administrative policies, and general harmony within school staff;
    (3) *community factors*—type (urban, suburban, or rural), population (foreign or native, heterogeneous or homogeneous), general level of culture, interest in educational matters, financial support of schools and cooperativeness toward school administration.
4. The norms of the tests are not the goals for all children to reach.
5. Realize that tests evaluate only part of the desired outcomes.
6. The tests should not be used for invidious comparison among pupils and schools.
7. If a teacher berates or scolds a child because of poor performance on a test, she may be building up unfavorable attitudes toward future testing.
8. Teacher failures that may affect testing and test scores are (a) failing to let a pupil know his results, (b) feeling insecure and threatened by test results, (c) being unsympathetic to the testing program and giving sarcastic references to it.
9. The teacher must realize that the testing activities contribute to the improvement of the child's learning.

10. Following an examination, it is proper and desirable to use test results in a class discussion of the items and interpretation of the results. (Individual results should be discussed with the pupil concerned.)

11. Do not disclose individual pupils' results in such a way as to permit comparisons among pupils.

12. Guard against the temptation of viewing the students as collections of test scores.

13. Review the student and/or class profile.

14. Seek the help of specialists.

15. Always consider that tests have errors.

16. Students with low scores may need special instruction and specific skill drill. Students with high scores will need enrichment.

17. If all other subtests are good and one is poor, it may indicate a lack of transfer of skills. Some skills are prerequisites to other skills.

18. Percentiles are probably the safest and most informative scores to use when dealing with the public.

19. Again, it is important to reiterate that the test results must be integrated with informal observations by the teacher, student's interests, grades received, and actual performance of the student.

20. Keep in mind that the only justification for the time and money spent on tests is that some beneficial educational results will be gained.

21. Test results should be used in association with other information concerning the student's background and environment.

22. The graphic presentation of a profile is one of the most helpful ways to analyze test results. The profile helps to make inter-individual comparisons with others of a similar category and intra-individual comparisons with examinee's own scores.

23. A single best occupational choice should not be inferred from the Occupational Interest Inventory.

24. Test results should be interpreted by competently trained professional personnel when they are to be used as a basis for decisions that are likely to have a major influence on the student's future.

25. The interpreter should constantly keep in mind what the test measures.

26. Comparable scores on two tests may not give comparable meanings.

27. Consider how the score will affect the person receiving the information.
28. Always consider that no test measures without error.
29. If available, local norms should be used in order to make comparisons with one's peers.
30. Individual conferences should be used to analyze personal test results. Group conferences should be used to explain the test program and basic test information.
31. Identify areas of strengths and weaknesses as revealed by average scores.
32. Parents have the right to know whatever the school knows about the abilities, the performance and the problems of their children.
33. Study guidelines for test interpretation provided by the District and the test publisher.
34. Hold meetings on test interpretation.
35. Provide for parental conferences.
36. Study all test results data carefully and use item analysis. Report for diagnostic and prescriptive purposes.
37. Be mindful of the fact that the tests are estimates of the variables measured and that they have errors and limitations.
38. Use the multiple sources available to supplement the interpretation of the test data.
39. Secure professional assistance for test administration and interpretation when needed.

## Notes

1. Henry S. Dyer, "The State Assessment Survey." Paper delivered to the Association of American Publishers, Washington, D.C., April 29, 1971 (mimeographed).

2. Henry Chauncey and John E. Dobbin, *Testing: Its Place in Education Today* (New York: Harper & Row, 1964), pp. 102-104.

3. Ned A. Flanders, "The Changing Base of Performance-Based Testing," *Phi Delta Kappan* 55, no. 5 (January 1974): 312. Emphasis added.

4. Lee J. Cronbach, "Mental Test and the Creation of Opportunity." Paper delivered to the American Philosophical Society, April 1970 (mimeographed).

5. Edmund J. Farrell, *Deciding the Future: A Forecast of Responsibilities of Secondary Teachers of English, 1970-2000 AD*. Research

Report No. 12 (Urbana, Ill.: National Council of Teachers of English, 1971), p. 141.

6. James W. Sabol, "Bellevue Public Schools, Specifications for Evaluation Strategy," in *Uses, Abuses, Misuses of Standardized Tests in English* (Urbana, Ill.: National Council of Teachers of English, 1974) out of print.

7. Susan Wood, *Evaluation of Published English Tests*, DPI Bulletin No. 144, Wisconsin English-Language Arts Curriculum Project (Madison, Wis.: Wisconsin Department of Public Instruction, 1967). This report was written under the direction of Robert C. Pooley, then a professor of English at the University of Wisconsin, Madison.

8. Oscar Krisen Buros, editor, *The Sixth Mental Measurements Yearbook* (Highland Park, N.J.: The Gryphon Press, 1965); and *The Seventh Mental Measurements Yearbook*, 2 vols. (Highland Park, N.J.: The Gryphon Press, 1972).

9. *Evaluation of Published English Tests*, pp. 85-86.

10. "Students' Right to their Own Language," *College Composition and Communication* 25 (Fall 1974). See this Special Issue for an analysis of the nature and implications of dialects, of the teaching of our "grammar," of implications for standardized tests, of the knowledge about language needed by teachers of English. Note also the bibliography of 129 entries.

11. For further information about the advantages and disadvantages of norm-referenced and criterion-referenced tests, see W. James Popham, "An Approaching Peril: Cloud-Referenced Tests," *Phi Delta Kappan* 55, no. 9 (May 1974): 614-615.

12. Robert B. Carruthers, *Building Better English Tests: A Guide for Teachers of English in the Secondary School* (Urbana, Ill.: National Council of Teachers of English, 1963). Available from ERIC Document Reproduction Service, ED 038 385.

13. "Some Things Parents Should Know about Testing: A Series of Questions and Answers," Test Department (New York: Harcourt Brace Jovanovich, Inc.), p. 4.

14. Alan C. Purves and Richard Beach, *Literature and the Reader: Research in Response to Literature, Reading Interests, and the Teaching of Literature* (Urbana, Ill.: National Council of Teachers of English, 1972).

15. Dallas, Texas, Independent School System, "Criterion-Referenced Tests," in *Uses, Abuses, Misuses of Standardized Tests in English* (Urbana, Ill.: National Council of Teachers of English, 1974) out of print.

16. For example, the New York State Education Department provides schools with "test-loan packets" to help them develop their own programs of standardized tests and thereby have samples of tests readily available to them (ETS *Testing Programs*, p. 31).

17. Dallas, Texas, Independent School System, "Checklist for the Administration of Standardized Tests," in *Uses, Abuses, Misuses of Standardized Tests in English* (Urbana, Ill.: National Council of Teachers of English, 1974) out of print.

18. Dallas, Texas, Independent School System, "Some Considerations for Teachers in Using Tests and Test Results," in *Uses, Abuses, Misuses of Standardized Tests in English* (Urbana, Ill.: National Council of Teachers of English, 1974) out of print.

## Afterword

*Alfred H. Grommon*

In this report by the NCTE Committee to Review Standardized Tests, Parts One and Two have been devoted to establishing some background about testing programs and to identifying trends in statewide programs of testing and assessment, particularly those trends that may guide English teachers and others in reducing problems posed by conventional uses of standardized tests. Part One, in particular, offers recommendations that may help teachers already involved in using standardized tests or in considering their use. The review of these matters and suggestions is intended to help teachers avoid some unnecessary difficulties arising from their considering tests somewhat in isolation or at least in a context too restricted to enable them and their students to derive benefits from whatever assessment program they are involved in. On the positive side, suggestions are offered for the improvement of testing, such as the creation of tailor-made tests or the emulation of an exemplary statewide program of assessment.

The major purpose of this report lies, however, in Part Two where readers are offered reviews of many published standardized tests, some of them in wide use nationally. Those reviews focus on the validity of such tests. The reviewers were concerned with the relationship of the content of each test to what is now known about the subject matter of English and about the treatment of particular aspects in English classes. They were concerned also about the relationship of that version of subject matter to the diverse cultures and learning styles represented by the wide variety of pupils. They were not concerned, however, with such other important features of standardized tests as reliability of items, nature of the sampling of test-takers, standardization of norms, treatment and interpretation of scores.

The ad hoc Committee was charged by the NCTE Committee on Research to devote its attention to commercially prepared and published standardized tests designed to evaluate students' command of the English language, grammar, usage, diction, spelling, the effectiveness of their written expression in English, and their knowledge of and responses to literature. Reading tests were not included.

As the distribution of reviews in Part Two indicates, most of the available standardized tests are intended to measure students' command of aspects of English grammar, usage, punctuation, capitalization, and spelling. Fewer tests are available to assess the ability to write English effectively and to respond to literature sensibly. Undoubtedly, English teachers already experienced in creating their own criterion-referenced or content-referenced tests fill in such gaps in standardized tests with their own means of evaluating their students' writing ability and response to literature. The Committee hopes some of the preceding suggestions and materials and the reviews of published tests may encourage other teachers of English also to venture into test-making.

Although the Committee made an extensive search for tests related to its assignment, it realizes that it must have inadvertently overlooked some that may be more valuable and even more widely used than those it was able to obtain from publishers. Some English tests, however, were intentionally omitted, particularly those used as a part of the National Assessment of Education Program and those used by the College Entrance Examination Board because those tests are not generally available to English teachers for their own purposes. Then too, given the time between the inception of the Committee and the publication of its report, it was inevitable that some published tests would go out of print or be so extensively revised that their original review was no longer applicable.

As an outgrowth of the programs of testing and assessment throughout the country, tests are undergoing revision, new ones are being created, and reports in the ETS surveys indicate that still others are being planned. Almost every state reported that the problem with top priority is the designing of new tests that are better suited to measure validly its educational goals, the educational programs of its local schools, and the diversity of its students.

Consequently, this present report is only an initial effort in the plans of the Committee on Research to provide the profession of English teaching with continuing reviews of standardized tests in English. Thus, periodic reviews of revised and new standardized tests in English, and of some that may have been overlooked in this report, are expected to be published by NCTE for the benefit of English teachers and their students everywhere. Furthermore, the NCTE has appointed both a Task Force on Measurement and Evaluation in English and a Committee on the National Assessment Educational Program. In the last twelve months, NCTE has published the report of the Task Force as *Common Sense and Testing in English* and the report of the Committee as *National Assessment and the Teaching of English.*

The contributors to this report sincerely hope their efforts are not only of some benefit to teachers of English, now and in the near future, but also offer a short cut to establishing a continuing review of standardized tests in English that are prepared by publishers to be sold to teachers of English.

# Index of Tests Reviewed

P 573

## DATE DUE

| | | | |
|---|---|---|---|
| | | | |
| | | | |
| | | | |
| | | | |
| | | | |
| | | | |
| | | | |
| | | | |
| | | | |
| | | | |
| | | | |
| | | | |
| | | | |
| | | | |
| | | | |
| | | | |
| | | | |
| | | | |

GAYLORD

PRINTED IN U.S.A